Thione NIANG

MEMOIRS OF AN ETERNAL OPTIMIST

"A personal story of perseverance,
triumph over obstacles and the power of a dream"

WASHINGTON **PUBLISHING**

This book is gratefully dedicate to my late grandfather Mame Thione

Mame Thione taught me how to be a man, humility, faith and kindness to all.

Mother taught me love and compassion. My children taught me responsibility.

Grandpa, I love you. I remember your pure love and care for me and will never forget. May you rest in internal peace.

CONTENTS

Part IV

Preface

oday, I am thirty-seven years old; my sons are growing and changing at an incredible rate, and they adapt to their fluctuating environment with great talent and intelligence. I watch them as they build their lives on very different models than the ones I had as a child. Sometimes I am confused, even baffled.

Frequent questions about my background over the years have helped me understand how my story is different, and even surprising. Yes, my life is atypical; born and raised in Africa, I spent twenty-two years in a small Senegalese town. My birthplace lacked many things, but was rich in others. Ultimately, though, it wasn't entirely able to prepare me for life in the United States, especially for my work with President Barack Obama. But, never do I forget where I came from. Today, I have dual nationality status, Senegalese and American, and a meaningful bicultural life, with a range of diverse experiences that I treasure.

The growing individualism in our societies, the "all at once" that sometimes seems to characterize the current generations, makes me think about what and who I am, what I can bring to the world, and how I can best contribute to enacting necessary changes. Multitudes of people desire and anticipate such change—people, who often face patterns of life preventing them from acquiring what is unjustly inaccessible to them.

Today I want to contribute to a better world, and I firmly and sincerely believe that to do so is not only possible, but absolutely necessary. Because my life has changed dramatically, because I believe in solidarity and sharing, because I have experienced the ways in which unity is strength, because participatory democracy is a sensible goal, and because we must help each other at all costs, I want to testify.

It is my ongoing projects and plans for future endeavors that motivate me and constantly remind me of my goals. The emergence of Africa, the continent finally realized to be full of promises and a bright future, as well as multiple projects involving the cooperation of the major players in African countries, fascinates and upsets me. This brings so much to my own life—from Kaolack, Senegal, to Washington, D.C. It is possible!

I have received so much from the people I've met and the places and circumstances I've experienced. For me, today is the time to create change and give back, taking the Give1Project to the highest point possible.

My goal is to identify and support young entrepreneurs and leaders across the globe, who nurture development and citizenship projects (such as the far-reaching goal of electrification for Africa), thereby improving the world for future generations—and there is certainly enough work to do!

By revealing the key moments of the examples and situations I've experienced, I hope to illustrate them as the sources of constant motivation that has enabled the evolution of my dream into reality. It is this that led me to write the following pages.

PART I

CHAPTER I

SAMA THIOSSANE

« As soon as you're born, you begin to die. » American proverb

The birth of a child is usually the fruit of a beautiful encounter between two beings. As days, months, sometimes years go by, the union of two loving souls deepens, and hearts are set on fire. From there is borne the desire to start a family. Beyond a proof of love, the arrival of a child often bears the wish for preservation, and even transmission. Two lines (of descent) are joined and embodied in a little person who will be the bearer of their story, a story that will live on well after their earthly passage.

In the tradition of my country, like that of many other nations, the objective of marriage is the junction of two family lines. The love between the two people involved is rarely a factor, and no one takes into account the bride's wishes. The consequences for her and her children are often very difficult to bear, as my story shows.

My father, Mustapha Niang, was a teacher in the primary school of Medina, a peaceful neighborhood of Kaolack in Senegal. One of the students in his Cm2 class (5th grade, the last year before middle school), a 15 year old girl, was a true standout. Amidst a buoyant and tumultuous ocean of kids, she was like a pearl. Quiet and poised, with delicate and graceful manners, Yacine Diouf caught the eye of her teacher. Her posture and maturity moved him. A hard-working and meticulous student, she always spoke to her teacher with respect, never really meeting his eye; yet she exuded self-confidence and serenity. Intoxicated by his desire to know her better, and hopeful of getting past her shyness, Mustapha decided that this young girl would be his. After all, she was from a good family that was religious, traditional, and highly-respected within the community. In his enthusiasm, he shattered the wall of propriety between him and his young charge by visiting Thione Diouf, her father and my grandfather, to ask for her hand. Fortunately, my grandfather, nicknamed "Mam Thione" by all, considered Mustapha a worthy suitor for his daughter. He was educated, stable, and already a husband and father. Hence, Mam Thione responded: "I will give you my daughter. All you must do to show your intent is offer me a few symbolic kola nuts, and she will go to you."

Two days later, the bonds of matrimony were tied between my father, a 35-year-old man who was already married, and my mother, a young teenager who became his second wife. In Senegal, marriage unions traditionally are negotiated and handled by the respective families, not by the bride and groom themselves. The man can sometimes choose his wife, but the woman never has a say in the process. In fact, she is often the last person to learn of her new marital status. Mam Thione told his daughter: "You are now a married woman and here is your husband. Over time, you will learn to love, respect, and obey him."

As is tradition, the wedding ceremony took place the very same day that my father asked for my mother's hand. The union between my parents was arranged, like many others at that time. Unions were first and foremost an alliance between two families for the purpose of creating descendants that would mirror their respective images: a progeny both honorable and valiant, the product of a perfect education.

That day, my mother, who was still a child, became a woman. Governed by the practices and usages of an age-old ritual, this moment was probably going to be the most important time in her life. She completed the preparation process in front of a group of women: cousins, aunts, mothers, sisters, friends, and neighbors, they were all there. In unison, they sang and praised the bride and her parents, and took great care to dress her in a white loincloth.

The ceremony took place in the afternoon, in the Medina mosque. Almost all of the guests were male. Tradition forbids men and women from mingling; therefore, the young bride, unable to see Mustapha before the sunset, remained in the house with the other women during the ceremony. As the service commenced, the fathers of the bride and groom gave their consent in the presence of the witnesses, and Yacine's fate was sealed.

For young Yacine, this moment served as an initiation into her new life. The circle of women around her, suddenly experts in marital relations, began to pass on myriad recommendations and hints about being a good wife. The recipe book for eternal bliss was sung, whispered, or calmly told by some, and delivered threateningly by others. Yacine had to focus in spite of the growing apprehension she was experiencing. A thousand questions crowded her young mind, making her dizzy. Fortunately, the preparation was almost over. In the mosque, the audience was already congratulating, and the [families of the bride and groom] happily offered the famous kola nut, a symbol of union and mercy, to all the guests.

At sunset, Yacine and her delegation began their procession towards Mustapha's house. Along the way, the assembly invoked the young girl's ancestors and sent forth prayers of blessings for the holy union of Yacine and Mustapha.

Once in her new home, the bride met and was welcomed by an assembly of new faces. The wedding party gradually left, and the eldest announced, "Here is your new family," before departing. Her hands clammy and her heart pounding, young Yacine took her seat in the indicated chair. Still in shock from being left behind by her own people, she fought back her tears and accepted a drink brought by a little girl. As soon as she took one sip, the Elder reappeared at her side to introduce her to Mustapha's first wife, her "Woudjou," or "rival." With a mischievous smile, the first wife delivered a never-ending litany of good wishes and welcoming words; however, Yacine noticed an unmistakable trace of jealousy beyond the veil of politeness.

After these formalities, the young bride, surrounded by her ever-present motorcade, visited the enclosure of her new house with Mustapha's first wife as her guide. She struggled to take in her new environment as her Woudjou half-heartedly shared the rules of the house amid a brouhaha of prayers, bursts of laughter, and boisterous conversations. Her Woudjou's lack of enthusiasm foreshadowed the blatant competitiveness to come. It was then that the young bride truly understood her fate. She had to comply with the rules of cohabitation, or she would endanger the family equilibrium. She had to integrate as quickly and smoothly as possible into a family that already had four children, and was to care for these children as if they were hers for half of each week. From then on, all that she owned would only be half hers: her house, her husband, her life, and her happiness.

All of these changes were brutal and sudden, and there would also be the household chores that were now her responsibility. Within a few hours, and in spite of her young age, Yacine became a wife, a rival, and a step-mother—heavy responsibilities indeed for a young girl of barely 15. She also had to face the daunting prospect of living and sharing a bed with her teacher. However, eager to become an exemplary wife, she followed the advice of her elders as best she could, and decided to surrender to the dictatorship of tradition. One year later, her son, Fallou, was born, the product of her union with Mustapha and her first contribution to the Niang clan.

Without delay, her firstborn went to live with his maternal grandparents to lighten the young mother's daily workload. This is a frequent practice in our culture. The closeness of the two houses made this separation tolerable, and later on, Yacine was even able to resume her education. In spite of her husband's reluctance, she managed to get a diploma in typing. Mustapha could not understand the point of this effort, and reminded her that she would not be allowed to work. It was a unilateral decision, since my father was not one to discuss things at length. Instead, he preferred to make all important decisions, and expected my mother to submit to his judgment. Any hint of a disagreement was not acceptable, since, per tradition, the couple had to agree at all times. It was in the midst of that dance, choreographed by our customs and passed on from one generation to the next, that I entered the world.

I was born on January 8, 1978, in the regional hospital in Kaolack. I was the fourth of the ten children borne by my mother. Our father's offspring would eventually total twenty-seven children, almost evenly distributed among three wives. At the time of my birth, my father was getting along exceptionally well with Mam Thione. Thus, in honor of my grandfather, he named me "Thione."

From very early on, my family provided a nurturing and loving environment. I had the same name as my grandfather, and I was one of his favorites. I was the "husband" of my grandmother, simply because I was also Thione; and even Mother would call me "Papa" for that reason. Grandfather was a good tailor, known for his taste and for the great fit of his creations. Although he was not formally educated, he was a resourceful learner, and he had perfected his art in the Ivory Coast. My mother and my aunts believe that my love of well-cut suits comes from Grandfather. He liked to buy Western clothing in Gambia, the neighboring country. At the height of his career, he owned nine sewing machines and employed a dozen workers. He trained a great generation of dressmakers in Kaolack, as well as in nearby communities. Unfortunately, I was born after this golden era.

My first significant steps onto the very long path of life took me, at the age of five, to the Koranic school of Médina Baye, a neighborhood in Kaolack; then to a French school, where the curriculum was much more varied. The school system served as a detriment to our national languages. The colonial rulers did everything they could to deprive the African people of their mother tongues. Teachers and staff at these schools considered speaking in Wolof, Toucouleur, or Sérère an alienating choice of expression, and they severely punished any student who used a local language while in school. Such offenders had to wear a donkey bone around their necks for an entire week, especially in the recess area. Donkeys, in Senegal as in other African cultures, are the embodiment of stupidity and inanity. This penalty, which students greatly feared, was a signal that the other students could make fun of the "guilty" student, whose shortcomings in French were pointed out for all to see. I would understand years later that those tactics were residual practices from the colonial era, when French settlers sought to spread the language of the "master."

In the El Hadj Ibrahima Niasse primary school, I was a diligent and hard-working student. The teachers had particularly high expectations of me because I was the son of the school principal. My father's rise to the head of the school had been fairly easy, and relatively expected, because he was ambitious. Beyond teaching, he wanted to play a role in bringing about positive change for his people in Kaolack. As a result, he was very involved in several political spheres, and was one of the most active militants in the socialist party.

Party meetings were always held at our house, which was located in the center of the neighborhood, and he often would represent the Mayor of Kaolack at these gatherings. As a small boy, I could see him juggle his position as a Council Member and his role as the school principal. Involved, always listening to his next of kin, he was available to whoever requested his help. When he had to attend important meetings, my brother, Bass, and I would follow him, pretending to be his bodyguards. In the commotion of political debates, there was always a risk of violence (led by the opposing party) targeting our father. I was only ten, but my brother and I were terrified by the idea that our father could get hurt.

Therefore, driven by a strange mix of bravery and madness, we would always escort our father though his campaign stops, in the presence of the Mayor of Kaolack. It was even more dangerous at night. Bass and I had developed myriad defense strategies to protect our father from possible danger. These nightly missions yielded moments of bonding and solidarity between the members of our family. I did not know it then, but this solidarity wouldn't last.

During this time, it was rare to become rich in the field of politics. At home, our entire family would cram in a plot consisting of three rooms over a few square meters. The physical closeness did not help alleviate the atmosphere of permanent conflict between the wives, nor did it mitigate the competitiveness between the children. Our mother, my brothers, and I were attacked from all sides. Our older siblings, children of the first wife, would rule the family to our disadvantage. Even though time has since healed many of those wounds, some memories still sting. To this day I remember the pain felt from one particular event.

It was the eve of Tabaski, often called the "feast of the ram." The celebration brought the same level of excitement, as does the Christmas holiday, when people young and old rejoice in the festivities. The entire area was absorbed in the preparations, which included a ram, decorations, gifts, and, most importantly, new clothes for each of the family members. New clothing was especially important to my siblings and I, since our mother used to say, "We will wear beautiful new clothes to go pray and start the New Year." The house had been in a state of ebullience for several weeks already. On this occasion, each man in the family had the honor and responsibility of "slaughtering" the ram that his family would eat on that glorious day. So, my father tackled the mission of finding the best ram; and found a strong, large, fat one, which in his opinion, would feed our household for more than a week! This claim seemed impossible, because we were more than 20, but I didn't dare to contradict my father and only watched, slightly amused, the attention he lavished on this rather slow and noisy animal.

My mother's Woudjou had hogged a corner in the kitchen to install a small box containing "her" dishes. "The flowers on my new bowls will give additional flavor to my cooking" she would say laughingly. I could see the endless comings and goings of all the members of our family, close or removed, and that of our neighbors. They were all giddy. Our small house was filled with laughter, conversation, banter, aromas, and spices, for the wives had already started to cook.

"Boys! My father shouted. Go to bed! Tomorrow will be a long day. We will go to the mosque for the Tabaski prayer. You must get some rest." The ceremony was to take place the next day, but too eager to know what gifts I would get, I didn't sleep very well. The next morning, I awoke at dawn, impatient to see my gifts. My father would probably give us a traditional outfit, but, being 12 years old, I was secretly hoping for a pair of Levi's jeans. I had mentioned them to my mother several times, because these jeans were very popular at school. Tiptoeing, I left my bed quietly, careful not to wake my brothers. I reached the family room, where our gifts were waiting, fairly easily. It was still dark outside, and the wind was blowing gently in the trees. I could hear the murmur of the leaves quivering, but I also heard another strange noise.

I could not tell where the sound was coming from, but I could someone sobbing nearby. "Who else could be up at this hour?" I wondered. The sobs were soft and muffled, but heavy and heartbreaking. My heart quickly realized who was suffering, and led me to the veranda, where I saw my mother in tears. She was sitting alone, her back bent, her head low. As I moved closer to her, she whispered, "Everything is fine, my son. Go back to sleep." I suppose she too had felt my sadness. She had recognized the pounding of my heart, a heart just like hers.

Unable to leave, I crouched next to her, without looking at her, and asked, Mother. Why are you crying? Are you in pain?"

She hesitated for a long time before answering, and finally said with a hurt voice, "I have nothing to give you or your brothers. You won't have new clothes like the others. You will get nothing. I have nothing to give you. Not even your Jeans."

I couldn't see her face, but I could see her tears splattering the floor and creating a small pool. That vision caused me great pain. No celebration, no clothes, no laughs could have made me happy if my mother was sad. "It's okay, Mother! We can wear our old clothes," I said.

"Yes, but one more time, your brothers and their mother are going to make fun of us. They always make fun of me, I'm used to it, but that they should laugh at you and ridicule you? I can't take it anymore, Thione."

"Don't worry, Mother. Maybe we won't have any new things to wear, but our faith, our humility and our respect for God will make us look our best."

Indeed, though we did not wear our beliefs on our backs, we wore them deep in our heart; and based upon that criteria, my mother looked the best of all. In my opinion she represented all the love, patience, and sacrifice in the world. She was a queen; she was my queen. To prove it, I made a promise to her. "Mother," I said. "I promise to you that one day, I will buy you new clothes for all the Tabaski celebrations to come. Happy Tabaski Mother."

"Happy Tabaski, my Thione."

From that day on, I felt partly responsible for my mother's happiness. Her dreams, her hopes, and her needs would be my guides in the dark waters I was going to navigate. As time passed, I felt all the more in charge because my father was overextended in all directions. He was the school principal by day and a politician by night; he was extremely busy and was often away at meetings and events. He was disconnected from our daily life and was unaware of the unhealthy, deteriorating atmosphere at home. Little did he know that hostilities between his wives were on the rise.

One day, my mother was busy preparing dinner for the entire family. Polygamous households are often organized around a sensible division of labor. In our home, each wife would prepare the evening meal and share the husband's bed twice a week. That day, it was my mother's turn to cook, and used, one of her rival's plates to serve dinner without first asking permission.

I was playing soccer with my friends when I heard my brothers' shouts. The entire neighborhood rushed to our house, alarmed by the screams, so when I entered the house, there was already a crowd. I was so alarmed that my legs suddenly become like concrete. I could barely move. My heart was beating too fast, and, fearing that it would jump out of my body, I tried to control it by grabbing my chest. Through my tears, everything looked fuzzy, and all I could see was my mother's body lying on the ground. In terror, I got closer and saw her lifeless in a pool of blood by the door of the hut that was our kitchen. What a dreadful vision. Thankfully, she was alive, but had been knocked out with an iron bar by my father's third wife, who quickly fled from the house to escape the overall indignation and any possible retaliation. My mother was barely breathing, and her whispers made no sense. Her survival, that day, was a true miracle: the local mechanic, the only person with a car, was able to drive her to the hospital emergency room, and she was rushed to the intensive care unit.

I ran behind the car over several hundred yards, until I could no longer see the vehicle. In my despair, I kept wondering, "What will happen to my Mother? What will I do without her? Why so much hate?"

This act of violence deeply traumatized and infuriated me, and led me to make, for the second time in my life, a decision without asking any parent. I decided to go live with my grandfather, where I would be safe and could escape such wanton violence. When he learned about my mother's injuries, my father initially had no reaction, but he eventually decided to leave the perpetrator of the crime, his third wife. However, to avoid additional tension within the Niang family, my grandfather opposed his son's decision and told my mother that "happiness in a household must sometimes take a thorny path." She had been trained to endure without fighting, to accept everything that her husband would impose. In return, she would enjoy a peaceful household and the paternal blessing would fall on her children. Once she returned home, the family took every opportunity to humiliate her and minimize her role within the family. This ostracization was exemplified when the family failed to tell her when my younger brother, Afè, was circumcised.

Circumcision is a ritual tradition practiced in the Muslim world. At 13 years old, Afé was going through this rite of passage to become a man. It is a happy event: everyone dresses in white to celebrate, and the circumcised individual is treated like a "little prince" all day long. For the mother, it is a day of both great fear and great pride. However my mother was denied the privilege of preparing for and enjoying this important event. She lived it as a witness, a passerby.

Indeed, it was only upon seeing Afè lined up in a procession of white-clad children that my mother understood that she had been robbed of the ability to participate in this unique moment in her son's life. Despite the injustice of the situation, she could not express any disagreement, since she could have been accused of failing her main duty as a wife: "to agree to everything that the husband says, decides, and does." So, my mother suffered silently, just the way she loved her children: silently. To this day, my mother has never told me she loved me, although I know that her heart was then, and still is, full of love for me.

In Africa, "love" is a feeling seldom displayed between parents and children. Who said that "emotion is black?" Although I was very fond of my mother, after I left, I would visit her house mostly to play soccer with my brothers. I felt like my true home was at my grandfather's house, where there was no competition among family. Also, for the first time in my life, I had my own bedroom. I was not the only one living at my grandfather's house, there were cousins too, and life was good.

Two years later, Grandfather was in a serious accident that left him paralyzed from the waist down. Afterward, we would have to help him move about and get to wherever he wanted to go, especially to the veranda, where he liked to sit early in the morning after the Fajr prayer. Every morning, my cousins and I helped him wash and change his clothes. I could feel that Grandfather was not comfortable with this kind of physical dependency. Sometimes he would get angry, and I could understand why: he was a prisoner of his own body. Although independent by nature, he could no longer do anything without his grandchildren's help.

In our culture, we do not believe in retirement homes; we live with our elders and accompany them with respect and gratitude until they reach their last haven. In good times or bad, we remain unblinkingly loyal to our relatives. What could be borne by a rootless tree, but a mealy fruit with a bitter taste?

In spite of this situation, Grandfather always did everything he could to take care of us, making sure that we had enough to eat, because hunger was a daily reality. Time and again, Grandfather and I wished for the unlikely generosity of a prospective visitor. When no such visitor would call, my grandfather would lend me his copper ring: a holy treasure, more than half a century old. Carrying the ring, I would go to the market in Kaolack to visit Seck, a merchant who was my grandfather's friend. With an empty stomach, but a heart full of hope, I would invoke my lucky star and pray that I would return to the house with food.

The ring was proof that I was actually sent by the old man, so that Seck could grant me a loan of 1000 CFA ($1). If he granted the loan, we could silence our hunger for the day—first the grandsons, then Grandfather. When he declined to provide a loan, we would simply surrender to God. The hunger in our bodies was like oil added to the fire of our faith, because faith manifests itself in all its glory only when we are stripped of the ephemeral. With his eyes shining, my grandfather would always tell me, "It is during hardship that your faith will be tested." More than once, this sentence helped guard me from the inertia of doubt, awakening in me the unquestionable conviction that my future would be bright.

At this point, my cousins, including my younger cousin Ousseynou, had dropped out of school, simply because buying even a pen was beyond our means. I can recount the number of months during which we had no electricity. During days of prosperity, I was able to do my homework by candlelight. More often than not, though, I had to learn my lessons as soon as I would arrive home from school, before sunset; and when the sun would set too early, Grandmother would wake me up at dawn the following morning so that I could study by daylight.

We also had limited access to water, and often had to shower with water drawn from the neighbors' well, which was truly a laborious task. The ablutions would end with tooth-brushing, not with toothpaste from a tube, but using a clever mix of salt and charcoal powder that was both more affordable and more available. We lacked money, so we had to be creative!

Nowadays, I feel entitled to consider some simple things to be obvious, a given, or "normal;" but I did not always have this perspective. In Kaolack, the word "normal" is not part of the vocabulary. Nothing is a given—there are no expectations, no disappointment. We were not dominated by our material poverty; rather, were reckoning in the freedom and spiritual strength that allowed us to hope that one day things would be better, simply by God's grace. Before worrying about material things, my cousins and I were primarily concerned about our dwellings. As a matter of fact, Grandfather's house, which was built in 1955, had a bad roof, and when it rained water would seep into the walls. Therefore, every storm, every hurricane, every disaster from the skies would make us pray and shout, "Today is the day! Surely the house will collapse!" However, just like our faith, the house would keep going strong.

On to the next storm, then …

In writing these lines and revisiting this period in my childhood, I explore the importance of cultivating the ability to adapt to one's environment from a very young age. Instead of being overwhelmed by a sense of frustration, I chose to accept and appreciate even what little I did have. Frustration only inhibits dreams and progress (material and educational in nature). Gratitude creates an opening for learning opportunities, an everlasting, and inalienable wealth.

CHAPTER II

A DAY UNLIKE ANY OTHER

« *As much as man is the father of the child, The child is the father of man* » *American proverb*

In spite of our precarious situation, it was nice to live with Mam Thione. We didn't always have enough to eat, but we were always there for one another. A kind of solidarity—a bond—had developed between us all as cousins, and we supported each other as much as possible. I felt good in my neighborhood, at school, and with my classmates. My peers even considered me to be something of a soccer star! As soon as the ball would hit the tip of my old sneakers, a sporty choreography would follow. My ball was an extension of my limbs: a kick here, a spin there, then up in the sky before a "chest-knee" control.

Over time, an ever-growing audience came to see me play. At first, it was mostly my friends, then some soccer fans, then girls. I noticed that during practice, girls liked to sit near the field, but they would not face us. From a distance I could hear them laugh, and I could see them whisper. Over several months, I ended up learning their names without ever talking to them or even waving hello.

At the time, I was not very interested in girls. I thought they were cry-babies and often spoke nonsense. But since I was now "popular," I had to be nice to everyone. I was often invited to their homes to visit on Saturdays and Sundays, and I would invite them to my home in return. Mam Thione's house often looked like a school recess area, because there were always so many people around.

"GIRLS AND BOYS! NOT. IN. THE. SAME. ROOM!!" Mam Diakhou, my grandmother, would shout from the kitchen.

Because I was a popular kid among my group, I seemed to have a small fan club that consisted mostly of local girls. Ousseynou and I didn't think much of it, but one girl in particular, Anta, always made me nervous. Anta was sweet, calm, and considerate. We were both shy, and were getting to know each other slowly, without rushing.

We saw each other twice a week, over the course of a year. Both of us were from very traditional families; and holding hands, kissing, or spending a week-end away together was simply out of the question. As a result, we dated slowly, one step at a time.

One beautiful Sunday morning in Kaolack, Grandfather woke up very early, as always, to go to the veranda near my bedroom. I would often watch him sitting in the shade, since the sun in Kaolack was very intense. He could stay there for hours, in total silence, listening to nature. The 78-year-old man looked, to me, like an angel, with the sun beaming on his white outfit and reflecting a blinding aura. I admired Mam Thione because he was my savior, my father, my guide, and a great source of inspiration.

It was during this peaceful contemplative moment that three figures appeared and broke the spell. Three women dressed in colorful boubous came in. They recited all their civilities and salamaleck to Mam Thione, then took place. At first, I saw nothing to worry about, but then I noticed that one of the women was Anta's aunt. "Was it really her?" I wondered. "Yes. No. No? Yes, it's her. It must be her," I muttered as I spied from my bedroom.

Anta and I had been dating for a year. She was my girlfriend, and I really liked her; however, we were not madly in love. Once—one time only in that entire year—we had spent the afternoon together, and that one time would bind our futures together, forever.

There I was, squatting, hands clammy, eyes set on these ladies. I broke into a sweat, and my ears were buzzing. Paying close attention, I listened to every bit of their conversation, barely breathing. My heart was beating so fast that I couldn't even think.

Thump, thump…Why were they there?…Thump, thump… What did they want?…Thump, thump…

"Anta is pregnant," her aunt said.

Anta…Anta was pregnant.

In the Senegalese culture, it is not the father or mother who personally delivers the news of their daughter's pregnancy to the in-laws. It is a mission for the aunts. These three words confirmed my fears. These three words meant that my future was going to take a sharp turn.

Though she sported a forced smile, it was obvious that Anta's aunt was very disappointed—her niece, who was, like me, only 16 years old, was pregnant. Upon hearing the news, my Grandfather kept his cool, then said, without flinching, "Thione cannot make a baby, he is too young for that." He didn't sound very convinced, and I felt terribly guilty, like a traitor or a murderer. I had just killed the hopes that my Grandfather had for me. I had just sacrificed my future on the altar of a precocious and unwanted pregnancy. In a country ruled by moral and religious rigidity, having a child out of wedlock, outside of the legal and religious conventions, was as terrible as a death sentence; but , marriage for us was out of the question.

Impassive, the three women recited the rules that Anta and I had to obey over the next nine months. "In nine months," said Anta's aunt, "Thione will be a Daddy. Tell him to get ready. During that time, he shall not see Anta. He shall not speak to her, and shall not try to get in contact with her. We will be back when the baby is born."

She pronounced those words in a clear voice, without hesitation. These were the instructions, or rather the sentence for my crime. I had never seen Mam Thione so disappointed. He had sacrificed everything for me since I was born. He was the only one who trusted me blindly, the only one who believed in my great future, and his esteem for me was now shattered. He had been investing in me for 16 years, and this was how I repaid him.

I would rather have become blind than to see the disappointment on Mam Thione's face. I would also have preferred to be deaf than to hear the terrible silence that surrounded him. That was the most painful thing: the silence. I wanted to disappear, to avoid his gaze. I thought about my mother, about the critics and teasing that she was going to endure from her Woudjous; and I thought about Anta. Because of me, she was going to have to stop studying, her future was in jeopardy, and she was going to be a single mother!

After the three emissaries left, Mam Thione, without looking at me, said nervously, "It can't be you, Thione. You are too young for this. It is not you." I answered with a long, shameful silence. Mam Diakhou, more talkative and down-to-earth, had a different reaction. She yelled at me, and clearly expressed her disappointment.

Anta's pregnancy brought an end to the hope and faith that my Grandfather and I had shared. We were already poor. How were we going to care for another innocent being? What had I done? Endless hours passed in terrible silence, with my eyes set on the little clock in the living room. What I dreaded most finally happened: we heard a quick, jerky footstep, and my mother entered Mam Thione's house. She stopped abruptly and looked for me. Her gaze caught me standing in a corner of the room, fidgeting with a button on my shirt.

With tears and questions in her eyes, she came close and begged me, "Tell me it is not you!"

I had just made her situation at my father's house even more uncomfortable. "Tell me it is not you! I beg you…" I kept silent, and my mother burst into tears. We cried together. We were crushed by our overwhelming emotions. She said that I was her father, her only hope, but I knew it was not true: I was 16, and I knew I was worthless.

When my father learned the news, he showed no reaction. He didn't lecture or threaten me; he remained impassive, stone-faced, and immediately started the preparations for the baby's arrival.

Every day, anxiety and unease would consume me. My soul, my heart, and my mind were in shambles. I had become a pariah among my classmates; I was a fallen angel. I was no longer a soccer star, but a criminal that people liked to judge. Days would go by in a string of insults. On the way to school, I could feel their eyes boring into me. A travelling court had been created, and each "judge" was sentencing me to a wide variety of sanctions, all increasingly cruel. The psychological pressure was at its peak.

In my social disgrace, I was overcome with self pity, but then I would immediately think of Anta. How was she? How were her days, her nights? What was she afraid of, worried about? Did she hate me? I wanted to ask for her forgiveness for all the harm I had caused. Questions about Anta were haunting me, preventing me from sleeping, eating, and living! Because I was not allowed to contact her, I sent my niece with a letter for the mother of my future child. But the letter was caught, and Anta was admonished even though I had sent it. To spare her from further trouble, I decided to keep quiet.

My life continued to take a turn for the worse. I used to be popular at school, but now my classmates were out chasing me. I tried to disappear entirely, to find solace and alleviate my depression and the self-hatred I felt. I disappeared to avoid dying of sorrow.

As days went by, I thought about how Anta's belly was probably growing and getting rounder. In a few months, an innocent little creature was going to call me "Daddy." Me, a father! The prospect of this new arrival was terrifying, because in the past few months, I had stopped perceiving the magic in the word "Daddy." My mind was plagued with endless questions: "Will I be good enough? What kind of father should I be…?"

The baby was born at the beginning of the following school year, and as planned, Anta's aunt came to get me. I went to her house to meet my child for the first time, and at last to see Anta again. When I arrived, a small assembly of older women left the room, and I saw Anta, sitting on a sofa with my child in her arms. As I approached, I saw the baby swaddled in a sky-blue blanket—a boy. I had a son! I smiled at Anta, with tears in my eyes, and she handed me her precious load. It was incredible! He looked just like my big brother Fallou! Eyes wide open, he examined me quietly. I was afraid to drop him or break him; but in his eyes, I could read his encouragement: "You're doing fine, Daddy. No, I won't break if you lift my arm. Yes, I see you. I see you counting my fingers and my toes."

Seeing my son calmed me. He was healthy. He was the result of an innocent union between two teenagers discovering each other, discovering life. Although traditional ceremonies took place very quietly, and with very little enthusiasm, I knew that my son, whom we had decided to name Bass, was a blessing. He was my child, my responsibility. I promised myself that I would honor him for the rest of my life. I wondered if my peers honor me in return. Now that I was officially a father, would they be nicer to me? What would become of a boy like me…?

In every circumstance, self-reflection is important to take a step back and analyze the facts and events. My experience reveals that avoiding impulsive reactions enables more favorable decision-making. I consistently force myself to reflect, explore and consider multiple perspectives in order to better understand the context of a situation. This method of proactive reflection has helped me overcome many obstacles.

CHAPTER III

BROTHERS WE ARE, BROTHERS WE SHALL REMAIN

"The golden rule of conduct is mutual toleration, seeing that we will never all think alike and we shall always see Truth in fragment and from different points of vision." Mahatma Gandhi

After disappointing Mam Thione, and bringing shame and disgrace upon my family, I felt orphaned and lonely. I lost my drive. All the things I used to love (playing soccer with my cousins, organizing events with friends) had lost their appeal. I couldn't eat, I stopped laughing, and I couldn't sleep. Even getting dressed was hard. "My shirt or my sandals? What should I put on first?"

Everything seemed difficult and useless. I was prisoner of my past; a prisoner of a mistake that no one in Kaolack would let me forget. I was on trial every day, and was bullied constantly, at school, in the street, and even at the grocery store. People would point their finger at me, in an accusing and mocking way. Even in the middle of a crowd, I was immensely lonely. There were no comforting words, no signs of understanding, no encouraging smiles, except from Mam Thione, who was by my side as I descended into hell. His support, although appreciated, was not powerful enough to make me forget the pain.

"Look, there comes Thione. The father-child with no family, and no house! His father probably disinherited him now that he has a kid. Look, he is still here! Why do you come to school? You have no future!" They chanted at me in unison.

A circled formed around me, and I was standing in the middle, humiliated by peers I thought were my friends. I was unable to move, and having neither the courage nor the strength to brave this last outrage, I surrendered. I decided to accept my sentence. I was now banned. I was a black sheep, a cursed child, unworthy of a home, a pariah to his peers. I drowned in a bottomless abyss, and my fall was quick, terrifying and painful. I had no desire to get up in the morning, or to speak with Mam Thione, although these conversations had always been my greatest and most beautiful inspiration.

In this way, I slowly became a hermit. I kept to myself in my room all day, and came out only at night, the only time of day when nobody could harm or slander me. At night, I could find peace. During these evenings, the wind seemed softer, the heat was less intense, the colors were less harsh, and the silence was soothing. I walked by myself in the darkness, aimless. Sometimes I would follow a cat, other times a soccer ball. I walked with my head bent as the streets became more and more deserted by the hour.

One night, during one of my lonely walks, I heard a song coming from afar. Walking in that direction, I lifted my head and saw a light coming from the mosque. In spite of my despair, I had no fear. It didn't matter where the light came from, be it a temple or a church, so desperate was I for shelter and support. I had nowhere else to go. Having lost my bearings, I could no longer rest on my usual pillars. I resolved to seek help in my faith--a source of unwavering serenity, comfort, and hope.

The mosque was close to my home, and attended by a warm, open community that knew nothing of my past. They followed the principles established by the late Cheikh Ibrahima Niasse. In Kaolack, I had received my religious education in a koranic school that he had previously founded. While visiting the mosque, I heard several people talk about Cheikh Ibrahima Niasse's travels around the world to places like Paris, Beijing, London, and Freetown— landscapes and civilizations that I could only visit in my dreams. I was entranced!

In Senegal, most Muslims belong to a brotherhood, or a group of believers, often with several million members, who obey the Sufi tradition. The brotherhoods all believe in the same general Islamic doctrines, but differ from one another based on the teachings of the specific Islamic scholar they choose to follow. There are several brotherhoods, but the ones with the most members adhere to the doctrines of Tidjanism and Mouridism. In Kaolack, these two groups were present in two different neighborhoods.

Medina Baye, my neighborhood, was now Tidjane, and the home of an important pilgrimage where you can meet people of many different nationalities, all there to study the Koran and

Tidjanism. Distinguished religious personalities come to pray with devotion. Amidst the tense atmosphere in Kaolack, one voice would calm my spirit: that of the muezzin calling for prayer. That voice seemed to talk to me only, urging me to leave my purgatory, and I was happy to take the three-minute walk between Mam Thione's house and the Great Mosque. I would go to the Mosque early in the morning to ask for God's forgiveness and a clear conscience. I was living in the Mosque, and the Mosque was living in me. My faith was my refuge.

At the mosque, I felt at ease, lighter, fascinated by the openness I experienced. After all I had been through, I longed for a different way to coexist with the world; another way to communicate with tolerance and respect. In spite of our differences, whether physical, linguistic, or cultural, weren't we all the same in the end? This question was constantly on my mind.

During this time, I felt the influence of Sheikh I. Niasse at various levels: in my neighborhood and at school, but also in my social circle. Yaye Khady Faty, herself the second daughter of the Sheikh, became like a second mother to me and treated me as her own son. In truth, she treated all of the children and youth in the neighborhood like her own, and we were grateful for that. Safe under her care, we would spend most of our time at her place. I was especially sensitive to the acceptance I felt in her household. They never talked about the brotherhoods, because I was a Mouride, and they respected my difference. I eventually became friends with Michiri Fall, Yaye Khady Faty's son. He often invited me to play soccer, probably encouraged by his mother to help draw me out of my depression. As time went by, Michiri and I became really great friends; and almost every night, I would have dinner with his family.

I always stayed after the meal to listen to Yaye Khady Faty recalling stories about her late father.

In time, I became Tidjane, not out of stubbornness or a desire to rebel, but out of faith and need. With the brothers, I found peace in my heart. The mosque of the Tidjanes in Kaolack provided the light I needed to guide me out of the darkness I felt. I did not consider my brotherhood with the Tidjanes an abandonment of the Mourides; I was simply getting in touch with myself, my beliefs, and my relationship with God. With them, I had found a way of expressing my faith that would help me exist in harmony with my environment. In my heart, I was not making a choice; as a believer, I was simply surrendering to and following God's direction. Maktoub: certain things in life have to be experienced, without the need for explanation.

Shortly after my conversion, I made my way to the Mosque with a light and determined spring in my step. On the way, I came across my half-sister, the eldest of my mother's first Woudjou. She was usually nasty to me and to my mother. Always on the lookout for a rumor, always smearing lies, her greatest pleasure was to make us look miserable to those around us. On this day, our eyes met for a fleeting moment, and I held tight to my rosary to prepare for her attacks. She wasted no time telling my father what she had seen: Me, with my rosary in hand, happy as a clam and looking very much like a Tidjane among his own kind.

My father was a pure-bred Mouride from the brotherhood of Sheikh Ahmadou Bamba. My mother was born and had remained Mouride. Even in the Tidjane area of Medina Baye, my father was well-known and fairly respected because he was the school principal.

When he found out from my sister that I had become a Tidjane, he summoned me and called an emergency family meeting. An assembly made up of all the family members gathered in the courtyard, to humiliate me, it seemed, in the best possible way: publicly.

My father first asked if the rumor was true; and when I confirmed its veracity, he gave me a choice: remain a Mouride, and remain his son, or become a Tidjane, and leave for ever. My decision was made, and so was his. "I disown you, I curse you, you will turn out badly because you have been a traitor to your own father." I was no longer his son, in spite of my mother's tears and pleas. Although I was aware that there would be even additional pressure on her for having borne me, "mbalitou fami bi," my determination was unmovable, my decision was final.

Faced with this curse, Mam Thione, himself a Mouride, told my cruel father, "I don't understand your anger at your son. He hasn't become a criminal, he has become a Tidjane; he is not going to jail, but to the Mosque. You should give him your blessing." Grandfather was livid, appalled, and in shock. Without lowering his gaze or blinking once, Mam Thione sought to fix the unfixable. He long waited for a gesture, a word, or a sign that would have reassured him, but my father didn't budge.

My decision to join a new brotherhood was a huge disappointment for my father, and felt he had no choice but to reject me. He had accepted the birth of my son, in spite of my young age, because he knew very well that I would one day become a father. It was the result of a precocious act, but not one that was completely unexpected. However, he could not accept that I would not carry on his Mouride heritage, in which he took great pride. My death would have been more honorable than my conversion. Once his decision was taken and final, I left my father's house for the second and last time.

With my conviction strengthened, I moved into the Mosque. I had to climb more than 20 stories of narrow steps to get to the little space I dared to call "my bedroom." Indeed, it was spare: an old shelf, a candle, and a thick blanket for a mattress, all inside a little cube whose opposite walls I could easily touch with my arms stretched.

In spite of the shabbiness of my dwellings, I felt privileged and grateful to have found shelter in God's house. It was especially hot up there, because I lived at the top of the minaret, where I could contemplate the beauty of the sun upon waking and the splendor of the stars at night. I was living in light that filled me and helped me shine beyond my dreams, despite the fact that my people had abandoned me in darkness. It was then that I began the process of Tarabya.

Tarabya is an exercise of total solitude that one undertakes only once in a lifetime, and the journey is meant to bring spiritual bliss. The exercise can take a week, a month, or even longer. The process, intimate and lonely, requires great concentration and total immersion in one's faith and beliefs. During the exercise, I focused on introspection and sought to let go of all the things, people, and events (recent or old) that could distract me. I spent my days and nights consumed by the purest and most serene pursuit of spirituality. I could even forgo food for entire days because my nourishment was spiritual.

My days were all the same: I would wake up and go to sleep at the same time. The only sounds to inform me of the passing of the day were the birds' songs in the morning, the call to prayer five times each day, and the chirp of crickets in the evening. This pace was only interrupted by the thoughtfulness of Yaye Khady Faty, who would have my supper delivered by someone who eventually became a good friend: Modou Diop. Modou's parents had let him live with Yaye Khady Faty so that he could learn the Koran. He was a bit older than me, independent, and very spiritual. He had already done his Tarabya, and after bringing me my food, he would always find a word, a tone, or a manner to encourage me. He was a tremendous help during my journey.

My immersion was total, and my focus was unwavering. Every day, I moved deeper in my Tarabya, to the point where I would forget my name, my house, and my family. I was no longer a son, a brother, a grandson, or a young father; I was one of God's many children in search of serenity.

My period of isolation lasted only one week, but it felt much longer for my mother and grandparents. To them, I had simply disappeared, and they were very concerned. It was too difficult for my Grandfather, crippled and without a wheelchair, to search for me, so my grandmother visited every neighborhood, every household, questioning neighbors, young and old: "Have you seen my grandson? His name is Thione," she would ask. After many fruitless inquiries, she began to panic. Despair set in, but she continued her mission of finding her little Thione. She found the energy to push on, and one rainy afternoon, her search eventually led her to the most unexpected place: the Tidjane mosque.

The day was hot, and the rain was torrential. It seemed like the sky was crying with joy, just as my grandmother sobbed with delight when she found me. She hesitated before hugging me because I had changed so much. My hair had grown a lot, and the shadow of a beard had appeared under my chin. My physical transformation was only the reflection of the newfound spirit of calm that dwelt within me. Serenity, stability, and strength from my Tarabya permeated my gaze, my movements, and my words. "Wipe your tears, Mam Diakhou," I said. "I'm fine. Let's go home and reassure everyone; but at dawn, I will leave again. I need a little more time."

Night had fallen, and under the starry sky in Kaolack, a young man was walking differently on the way to his old home. Was he taller, or was it his gait? The difference was not the result of any physical change, but of a spiritual calm that enveloped him. As he walked, he listened to the wind and experienced the coolness of the evening. For the first time, he was listening to his destiny.

Once I arrived at home, I reassured everyone with a hug, a smile, and a wink. I was happy to see them: they had not changed. Grandfather sat in his veranda, Mam Diakhou chatted with the neighbors, and my cousins played soccer. Everything was the same, suspended in time; everything, that is, except me, because I had become several years older within a few weeks.

As planned, I left at dawn the following day, and returned to my little cube at the Mosque. I had found my balance, and I could resume my examination of my past and my present. I was deep in thought when I heard a familiar voice, "Thione! It's me your Mother! Come home with me, my son! Please! I am living in hell at home. Stop this immediately!" My mother had heard of my short visit to Mam Thione, and had come to beg me to end my Tarabya. To convince me, she informed me of the death of one of my good friends, Laye Bamba, asking me to go visit his tomb to say good-bye. She told me about her difficulties and the increasing cruelty she experienced within the Niang clan, because my decision to be a Tidjane was unbearable to them. Because I was away, they took their vengeance out on her. She told me everything, as if she wanted to transfer her pain to me; but I did not accept it. I was hurting for my mother, my brothers, my blood, but I also had to remain loyal to my decision. With my conviction deeper than ever, and a twinge in my heart, I refused to follow her and continued to pursue my Tarabya.

Once my Tarabya was over, I was more and more attracted by all the unknown things found in me. People who are not familiar with the concept of "brotherhood" may think that they are only sub-groups of a single religious family; but there are strong rivalries between the members of the various brotherhoods that extend to all levels of society, from the family unit to the political arena. Usually, children are in the same brotherhood as their father, and the wife follows her husband. Any decision outside of that social framework is considered rebellion, but the perpetrator is not always disowned.

I often wondered about the real motives for the differences between brotherhoods; because, regardless of our membership, we are all brothers and sisters. We are "one." In my eyes, our differences should not make us hate each other. To the contrary, they should enrich our relationships. When I joined the Tidjane brotherhood, I was not interested in a denomination, but in the need to build myself and become anchored to something sturdy that would help me find my direction in life. Before my Tarabya, I felt unhappy, powerless, lost, and rejected by my own kind. Finding my way back from those dark emotions was a difficult journey, but after my Tarabya, I was ready to take on the world. I decided to return to my academics, and began preparing for the Brevet tests that were approaching rapidly.

The brevet is an exam that tests students' mastery of everything they learned in school to that day. What if I didn't pass? The possibility was torturing me. But luckily, it was only a small test compared to what I had already been through. All I had to do was channel my anxiety and take a step back. My father was sure I would fail, because, as he liked to say, "The path to disobedience does not lead to glory." Lacking outside support, I isolated myself in my faith and focused only on my determination to pass the exam with flying colors. Besides, I was not completely alone, because day and night, Yaye Khady Faty was protecting me with blessings and prayers.

When the exam results were published, I told her that I had passed. She stood up, hands to the heavens, and said, "God is great!" I realized that in Kaolack, there were those who prayed for me, and those who thought I would fail. My father, alone in his own category, was formidably indifferent. "I don't care," he said, rather disappointed that my half-brothers had failed.

I felt sorry that he felt indifferent, but it did not change the strange rapport between him and me. I still felt for him a truncated, battered, but ever-present love. Maybe I was already extremely tolerant, or maybe I was still naïve, hoping that he would one day "forgive" my choice of brotherhood. Maybe I was hoping that over time, obscure things would come to light. I thought that time would help my father and my family understand the true reasons behind the decision of a lost young father only 16 years old.

I would like to dedicate this paragraph to all those who believe in a divine entity, and especially to my Senegalese brothers and sisters. You can, better than anyone, understand the meaning and weight of our religious and social traditions. For this reason, I want to share my experience with the utmost sincerity. I was born Mouride, raised Mouride, and now I am Tidjane. Mouridism and Tidjanism have always been a part of me. On the path to my true spirituality, these principles have been with me for better and for worse. It is not my intent to prescribe or recommend this path. In the circumstances that were mine at sixteen, I was in search of my stronger, more confident self. This need prompted me to look at the world differently. In its contradictions and nuances, the world has attracted, surprised, shocked, deceived, and comforted me; but above all, it has taught me some of the most important lessons of my life. Over the years, after many travels, I can confidently say that we are all the same. Regardless of our confession of faith, we all believe in something greater than ourselves. We all crave the same things: respect, peace, tolerance, and love. Laws, beliefs, and morals are structures that help us live together and respect one another. Therefore, together we all make up a family united by ties that bind us more closely than our religious or cultural differences. If I had to choose a single, all-encompassing belief, it would be that of listening and tolerance.

PART II

CHAPTER IV

DAKAR

"High grass can swallow guinea fowls, but it cannot muffle their cry. "
African proverb

The social and psychological quarantine that I was experiencing in Kaolack was a worry for Mam Thione. He could see the tears in my heart. He suggested that I go live in Dakar at his sister's, Mam Khadi. I took a month to get ready. He sent me to borrow 1000 Fcfa from Kebe, a merchant, to buy a bus ticket to the capital. In the presence of my mother and my grandmother, he had me sit down and gave me his blessing, with sobs in his voice. Mam Thione's words and his sadness to leave me made me weak. The plastic bag in which I had packed my things slipped from my hands and broke open. I needed a bag but didn't have one.

Questions were crowding my mind: How would Mam Thione move around in my absence? How would he shower without my help? Who would go shop for him at the local merchants'? With whom would he reminisce about the colonial era and his glorious career as a tailor?

As if he could read my mind, the old man spoke to me. With eyes full of tears and an attempt to smile, he said, "Sit down, Thione, sit so that I can speak: never forget your mother's difficulties. She counts on you tremendously. Knowing that you are far away is an enormous sacrifice, so you will have to be useful through your work. You have the responsibility and the power to change your family's living conditions. I trust you; I know you will do it." At that moment, his voice broke: he pretended to cough, but I knew he was in pieces. According to my mother, I have the same sensitivity as my grandfather. I suppose she refers to his ability to cry. The old man knew that he was going to miss me. By deciding to let me go to Dakar, he too was sacrificing my presence near him.

I left my family, accompanied by my cousin Ousseynou. After a 45-minute walk, we were at the bus station. I made Ousseynou promise that he would help Mam Thione. I was leaving Kaolack and its brilliant scenes of misery, its crowds of children in rags…a town so dear to my heart. Although I was sad to leave my loved ones, I was happy to discover new horizons. I was on my way to Dakar. I was only 16-years-old, but I already needed a new life. In Dakar, my mistakes would not be judged. My intent was to study with a monastic commitment. I would fulfill my grandfather's dreams; my dreams.

In Senegal, the owner of a bus always writes a sentence on his vehicle to express his belief. The verdict that day, far from the "Alhamdulillah " that you read everywhere, sparked a fire in me: "When the going gets tough, the tough gets going" -- John Fitzgerald Kennedy. This quote reverberated in me unexpectedly and reinforced my decision to leave my family. For me, it was tough to keep going. But I wanted to keep going, and I also wanted to be tough. It was probably a sign! It meant that there was light at the end of the tunnel.

Once in Dakar, I found shelter at Mam Khady's. She lived in a little house on a dark and filthy pedestrian street. Medina is the most popular neighborhood in Dakar; Senegal's version of Harlem. The irony of my situation is that the Medina area was created by French governor William Ponty to house the black populations ousted from downtown Dakar following the plague epidemic in 1914. I–the plague of Kaolack–was taking refuge there.

My move to the city was also driven by the opportunity of a scholarship to study at the Japanese technical high school. Admitted students were offered a three-year education in Dakar, and then the possibility to get a diploma to continue studying in Japan. Why not? In Japan, there is an unmistakable business-like energy, which would mean the chance to find a good job and care for my mother. My motivation stopped there. I was leaving, because for me, and millions of African kids like me, leaving meant succeeding.

I had taken the exam in Kaolack three months prior and was fortunate to receive the scholarship. Now in Dakar, feeling happy-go-lucky, I was on my way to meet one of the principals at the Japanese school. He received the news of my arrival half-heartedly, and with slight discomfort. I understood later why he lacked enthusiasm; because of my late arrival, my scholarship had been offered to someone else. I wanted to argue and explain that I had not received their letters, that the tardiness was not my fault, and that the scholarship should have been for me, but I couldn't speak.

That day, under Dakar's punishing sun, I felt cold. And in spite of the blinding light around me, I felt darkness. For me, the horizon was out of reach. Prospects were suddenly less serene, and my Japanese dream was crumbling. "I would have to go back to Kaolack…". It would be chaos. This thought was killing me, but I couldn't give up. Going back to Kaolack meant that I would forgo my future, my mother's future, Anta's future, and that of my son, who had not even asked to be born. I was not registered in my school in Kaolack, nor in Dakar. In any case, even if there had been room for me, I knew too well that I had no money or financial backing to further my education.

One of my maternal aunts, Hadja M'bodj, was also living in Dakar. Upon the news of my arrival in town, she immediately refused to host me. She had decided to side with those who criticized me because of my brotherhood conversion. She was mocking me, and her husband was continuing the defamation campaign started by my father, that "I was a cursed child". Needless to say, none of them thought I had a great future. She had refused to be there for me when I needed her. But when I didn't need her, she would appear. She would check off the option "Return to Kaolack" box. My mother often listened to her, and this aunt's opinion could very well mean the end of my city adventure. My fears were confirmed when she tried to convince my mother that I would join the Dakar mob and become a delinquent if I didn't go back to Kaolack.

I wrote a letter to my mother to explain how noble my intentions were. I knew that my written plea would have a more emotional effect than any oral cry. In my plea to Mother, my words were reassuring. I organized and lobbied for my endeavor. I received support from my uncle Pap Diop –son of Mam Khady and my grandfather's sister–and from my older brother Fallou. Both spoke to my mother to convince her of my good faith: I would go forward and make her proud by being successful. Fallou–who worked as an attendant at a gas station and was making barely $90 per month– promised my mother that he would register me in high school in Dakar, and that I would keep studying.

Mam Khady's house was a typical Senegalese house. Apartments face one another, and you could witness the neighbor's domestic squabbles from your bedroom. This architecture reflects the Senegalese way of life, placed by large gatherings around big plates of Tchep djinn or mafé, where everyone dips their hand. People live in the same area, eat from the same plate, and practice their survival techniques. At Mam Khady's, I was given a room that was previously a storage room. It was the only room available. For my teenager size, it was the minimum possible in terms of space: one and a half meter over two meters. Three-square meters to put away the little clothing that I had, sleep and live. Live there, can you imagine? My dreams and bright future that I had invented for myself only lived in my head. In reality, my new urban days were scorching and smoky. The Guinean couple who lived across the hallway were always creating both, Senegalese and Guinean dishes and natural teas that sent flavorful smells throughout my new home.

The school year was already in session, and finding an available spot in the sophomore class was not easy. In Lamne Gueye High School, the Principal was very clear; there was no room for me, and he would not assist. My mother was paying a high price within the family, and now I was going to become a young drop out for lack of space in a high school.

Today, when I witness young people from various countries struggle with despair and envision suicide as their only option, I am glad I didn't reach that point. Maybe in Africa we have a slight advantage in that we are used to considering several solutions when we have a problem, before giving up and numb us with pain and despair. Suicide is not a choice, but a desperate act taken in a moment of weakness in the sole desire to end one's suffering. I thought myself lucky to have a humble vision of the world; which simply believes that "poverty is better than death". When I think of the thousands of youth who commit suicide every year for due to the economic struggle and other reasons, it breaks my heart. Maybe with more time they would have seen a little light at the end of the tunnel.

In the neighborhood of Medina, at Mam Khady's house, days went by. The cards of my fate were shuffled again, and I needed an ace to exit this dead-end. Every morning I would walk from Medina to the French Cultural Institute in Dakar–approximately three kilometers–while waiting for better days, and fighting my depression. My walks were not intended for city discovery or exercise like most. I faced the challenge of affording public transportation. The 'rapid bus', the cheapest means of transportation, cost 10 cents, and that was more than I could manage at the time. But I found solace in my walks; I acquired a fair knowledge of African literature during these weeks of idleness. Everyday at noon , I was supposed to go home, because in my house lunch was served to everyone at the same time. All gathered around a single large plate, and if you were not at home exactly at mealtime, no one would wait to eat with you. In spite of this constraint, I would stay in town to avoid too much walking, and would only eat in the evenings.

This was a decisive period in my life. If I had let my guard down and completely lost hope and allowed the little flame deep down inside me to burn out, I would have never pursued my studies and would not be where I am today. Even in doubt, fear, and uncertainty, there is an opportunity to grow. The key is to stay strong, recognize obstacles as opportunities, and to seize them. It is vital to remain confident in yourself.

CHAPTER V

TONTON SORANO:
A BEAUTIFUL ENCOUNTER

"One hand does not applaud." Wolof proverb

One Monday afternoon I was exhausted and walked aimlessly in the city. I remember all those mornings when, for over a month, I would walk with my eyes on the bluish horizon of Dakar. I walked trying to imagine what my future would be, but there was nothing, it was like watching a movie with no picture. My books were my shelter, ideal for traveling, discovering, escaping my daily emptiness.

I walked, hungry, my heart full of sadness, and my head in the clouds. Although I was tired, some superior energy was leading me as if this power knew better than me what my destination would be. This energy was the call of my destiny. I decided to stop near a public table near the Sorano Theater in Dakar where young people were having traditional tea. A little cup of tea was 50 Fcfa. Even if I had such wealth, I wouldn't have spent it on tea.

Since I was new to Dakar, I sat among the young tea drinkers to hear what was happening in town. These public places are almost universities because they are places where you come across all kinds of people, regardless of social class. From the conversations typically revolved around thoughts on philosophy, politics, the economy, or even history. All humanities met there. Maybe even the stimulating virtues of Senegalese tea at community gatherings would be revealed some day. That day, I borrowed two books from the library, The Discourse on the Method by French philosopher René Descartes, and Ambiguous Adventure by my fellow countryman Sheikh Hamidou Kane. Listening to people talk over tea was like reading a book. You learn a lot in a happy atmosphere.

As soon as I settled, I found myself impressed by a man who joined the group. There was a particular kind of energy that surrounded him and immediately I liked him. Simply upon seeing him, and not knowing why, my heavy angst lifted a bit. This person with the unique energy knew everyone except me. "You, I don't know you, what's your name?" he asked. "Thione. Thione Niang," I said. Seeing that I was not drinking, he offered a round and tea was served to everybody. It was my first drink since earlier in the morning, and I was grateful. His offering was greeted with many 'dieuredieuf'. Conversations picked up again: topics were ranging from the latest decisions by President Abdou Diouf, to the most recent album by Youssou N'dour, the local music star, and many personal anecdotes here and there. I remained silent, I had come to observe and listen to those around me. The gentleman with the special energy called me again, puzzled by my silence: "You seem to be worried, young man, what's wrong?"

I briefly told him about my embarrassment for not being able to carry on with my studies. He browsed through Ambiguous

Adventure, the novel I picked up earlier at the library and joked "your adventure is no less ambiguous". I smiled.

The author of the novel, highly respected Sheikh Hamidou Kane whom I met years later, confirmed that the book had left a mark on several generations who keep identifying with it. "Every year I receive tens of letters from students all over the world, who, although they are not from the peulh ethnicity like my characters, identify with the main character. This book is studied in universities, including by the Mormons of Utah in the United States. I was invited there in 2010 for a seminar about Ambiguous Adventure. There, Mormon students testified about the impact of this book on their personal life." Sheikh Hamidou Kane told me in November 2012.

The man with a particular energy had a sense of humor. But not only that! With compassion and understanding, he said he could help get me back in school. "Do you know the Lycée Lamine Guèye?" Was he testing me? That school is one of the best known in the country and had educated several generations during the first few years after the independence. He was surprised when I said they informed me that there was no room for me. After we drank our tea, this man with positive energy, whom all the kids called Tonton Sorano, asked me to follow him. He brought me to the Theater Daniel Sorano of Dakar. When we arrived at the national theater, Ibrahima Diakhaté, alias Tonton Sorano, everyone wanted to say hello and talk to him; he seemed like an important person. On the fourth floor, the size of his office reminded me of my tiny room in Medina. It was a little room with just a small table and two chairs. Sorano gave me a tour of the theater and showed me the vast auditorium, which impressed me greatly. "It is not for nothing that we call it the Great Theater," said Sorano. After the short visit, we went back to his office, and he made a phone call. He spoke with Monsieur Djeye, the principal of Lycée Blaise Diagne. "I have my nephew from Kaolack, who can't find a school in Dakar for studying in Second, could you…" He hung up, with a big smile on his face like a birthmark. It was a good sign that he would still be smiling after the phone call. "You will go to school. The principal of Lycée Blaise Diagne wants you to see him tomorrow morning".

My emotions were beyond joy and euphoria; it was more like a burst of fever because this new situation was brightening my dull horizon with a new coat of happiness. Although I was still in the dark about my future, I could tell that a new chapter was opening for me. I was experiencing the relief of a man who had been shouting for help in a dense forest, and who was finally hearing a comforting answer just as his voice is beginning to fail. Before Sorano, I was close to thinking, like Franco-Algerian writer Faïza Guène and numerous young Africans: "We worry about our future, but we shouldn't, because most likely we don't have a future".

The encounter with Sorano helped me find hope again; I cried, moved to discover that man could still be humane. That night, Sorano, who was then Program Director for the theater, explained that it was essential to help out. In fact, it was the reason he had met the principal of Lycée Blaise Diagne one year before. He described how they met: "He wanted to buy tickets to a show for his wife and child. The ticket clerks told him there were no more tickets to sell, which was true. But he seemed to want to see that show. After many tricks, I had gotten him three tickets. He meant to pay for them, but I said that a 'Thank you' would be enough". To Sorano's spontaneous kindness, I owe my returns to school, to life and my future.

Sorano had a great mind. That day he told me, still with a big smile, "Difficulties are as necessary as vitamins. Without them, you don't grow up. What matters is to remain positive, to believe in yourself, because you lose nothing when you fight". He was like a coach in personal development, and his professional path was in itself an illustration and a call to effort. He had been decorated Great Knight of Personal Merit at age 19 by President Léopold Sédar Senghor, because he had participated in organizing the first festival of black arts in Senegal in 1966. That first event for African black art held April 1st – 24, had been attended by various personalities such as Aimé Césaire, Langston Hughes, Jean Price-Mars, Duke Ellington, and Joséphine Baker.

Sorano—Ibrahima Dakhité by—had started his career in this temple of entertainment as a Xerox boy, before climbing the ladder to become stagehand, manager of the mailroom, then Programs Director, which made him number two of the vast theater of Senegal. However, Sorano had not even graduated from High School. "These degrees!" he would say mockingly, meant nothing because, in his opinion, the real diplomas in life were the blessings of one's parents. "When the parents' prayers accompany a child, there is no room for failure," he said, full of certainty. This brought me back to my father's curse, but the thought of my mother eased my pain. It was not a day for being sad.

After this conversation, Sorano, who had a paternal instinct, realized that I was hungry. He walked me back outside and gave me a 500 Fcfa coin. The first thing I did was to run into a joint to buy some food, and then to take a bus home, my heart filled with joy.

From this encounter, I would later learn that the best things in life are often unexpected and that they often happen thanks to unexpected people.

At home, my situation of quasi-dropout was not a worry for my aunts. Young men with no education were not rare in the family; on the contrary, it would have been exceptional. Assuming that the news of my going back to school would not impress them, I said nothing at all. That night, after dinner, I organized my belongings with great care. I fell asleep; confident that tomorrow would be another day.

My conclusion of this period: never deprive yourself of the possibility of meeting new people. Don't hesitate because of shyness or misunderstanding. When referred to meet someone, realize it is a sign of trust. Today, we refer to this as networking. Seize every opportunity, even those seemingly unrelated to your main objective. Unexpectedly meeting Tonton Sorano and subsequently entering high school is an example of this in my life. Know how to recognize a helping hand and accept the unexpected. Who knows what could happen? Some say every network starts with the storekeeper next door.

CHAPTER VI

BLAISE DIAGNE HIGH SCHOOL
& THE ENGLISH CLUB

"Together we will work to support courage where there is fear, foster agreement where there is conflict, and inspire hope where there is despair." Nelson Mandela

At dawn, when the rooster sang, I woke up, prayed and got ready quickly. For months, I had rehearsed and refined my new routine in my head. No time to eat, no time to lose for these kinds of niceties.

Once in the Lycée Blaise Diagne, I noticed that the recess area was not as empty as the one in Lycée Valdiodio N'diaye in Kaolack. There were young people everywhere; they were talking, laughing, teasing. It was as lively as a beehive. They seemed to be sure that no cloud would disturb their horizon. They had a future, and I was envious.

At the school office, they asked me to wait for the principal who would green light my attendance. When the bell rang at 8:00 am, signaling the end of recess outside, I heard the students' clamor die down. Serious things had started without me, one more time. When the bell rang at 10:00 am, I was still sitting on a chair in front of the administrative office waiting for the principal to show up. The students' clamor resumed, faded again, and yet I remained.

Five minutes later, a short man, dressed in a Senegalese kaftan and a white hat, walked authoritatively in the direction of the office where I was waiting. "How are you, young man? Are you Ibrahima Diakhaté⊠s nephew?" he asked. I nodded, and he led me into his office. He called his assistant over the intercom and gave her a written recommendation so that she could introduce me to the Dean. The latter was out sick, so began my wait once more. But my patience was running out and my eagerness to begin class was growing stronger. Upon hearing my plea, the Secretary authorized me to start my day.

It was a Tuesday, and the Second grade in Lycée Blaise Diagne was studying English. The teacher, Carine Lawson, was an American volunteer: a real American with the right accent! She was a beautiful woman with an Asian face. I had dreamed of going to school, and now my dream featured an American teacher. Carine Lawson took attendance and said that those who had not heard their name were to say it. Expectedly, I didn't hear my name and explained that I was not yet officially "in", yet she let me stay in class.

It was one of the first English classes of the year. The teacher told us about American culture. She explained in America there are values that encourage excellence; American parents say to their children– from infancy on–that they are intelligent. They encourage them and tell them that they are the best and can succeed at anything. Regarding the need to work relentlessly, Carine Lawson explained that most Americans eat in fast-food places, to spend less time in restaurants. They had developed the habit of eating while working, without a break for rest. For Carine, it was also essential to serve one's country and mankind, and this is why she had volunteered to teach English in Senegal. Her commitment, she said, helped her country expand its influence in the world and connect with remote people. My understanding developed past my need to give to others around me as I absorbed her words. How could a country place the need to succeed at such a high level of priority? I couldn't help but to compare this portrait of an American parent with that of my father. Then I thought about my mother, and the need for me to succeed to support her… America already embodied what I wanted. In Kaolack, our English teacher in 8th grade often spoke about Koffi Annan, then Secretary-General of the United Nations. Why not become the next Koffi Annan? I listened to Carine Lawson, and ideas rushed to my head. I must go to America; I need America.

The teacher told us about an English club in the school and encouraged us to register to improve our language capabilities. When I went to see her after class to find out how to enter this club, she sent me to her Senegalese peer, Monsieur Diop, who was spearheading the club. The following day, the Dean was there, and my registration became official. With the intent of registering in the English club, I went to the teachers' room to meet with Monsieur Diop. Like everywhere else in Senegal, there were several Messieurs Diop, I was told. "Monsieur Diop of the English club," I said quickly to not lose any more time. He saw me, and although he said that club activities had not resumed yet, he promised to enter my name on the members' list.

After midday the classes were over, I went back to see Sorano to express my gratitude. He had become my friend–someone I admired. Once or twice a week I would go to him. Thanks to him, my life was starting to feel normal. My mother and my uncle Pap Diop, as well as Mam Khadi, were relieved to see me back in school. I would walk from Medina to the Amitié (Friendship) neighborhood, approximately 2 kilometers, and walk back home for lunch, logging 4 kilometers daily under the strong Dakar sun.

Two weeks after going back to school, I noticed by chance, a group of kids who were speaking English fluently at recess. I approached them to find out how they could speak English without any accent or difficulty. Somebody said it was thanks to the English club, where they belonged since the previous year. They had even named an area in the courtyard the "London Corner," a place where you could only speak English.

The English club resumed a few days later, and I was able to progress, as I had wanted. I was quite taken aback at first, but soon I longed for Wednesday afternoons like a farmer awaits rain with impatience. Since there was no class on Wednesday afternoon in our school schedule, we could indulge in our joint passion: English.

The English club held class from 12:30 pm to 4:00 pm. I had a choice between going home for lunch with the family, or skipping lunch to partake in the club activities. Saying "choice" is just a way of speaking of my desire to know Shakespeare's language was growing stronger every day. Beyond the rules and grammar that we learned, the club was busy writing and producing speeches, engaging in dialogues between members, and creating songs, skits, and text commentaries. "For this new school year, we must put our club under the leadership of a new team. We must elect a club board, people with a vision who will be able to create a new impulse for our organization", said Monsieur Diop gravely.

I was thinking of being a candidate, although I was only the latest addition whom no one knew. I thought that even if I didn't win, I wouldn't lose anything either. I would at least make friends.

Out of the 50 or so people in the club, one member named Sogui stood out. He had been very active since the first sessions and well known within the group. He was a candidate for the presidency, but other positions were still open such as: Vice President, Treasurer, and PR Secretary. I asked Sogui which position was still available in his circle, and he said he did not control who would want the opening of PR secretary, but that he would support me for it if I wished to be a candidate. This providential alliance was perfect for me.

I was savoring, for the first time, the sweet taste of electoral success. It had been too long since I had belonged in something. Less than three weeks after my arrival at the Lycée and just a few days after entering the English club, I found my place quite satisfactory. It helped me fully integrate into the organization and the lycée. New energy was now spreading throughout the group with the assistance of the new members. We had daily work sessions at recess to help our progression.

There were other specials clubs that students joined such as Philosophy, Latin, Spanish, and French. But the English club was gaining momentum by organizing speech contests between the various English clubs in other schools in Dakar. We were "the debaters" before actor Denzel Washington. I was studious in class, I was betting on my future and my family's future. My life at the time was revolving around a trilogy: my books, my rosary and my struggling companions, my brother Fallou and my friend Amadou.

No cloud could darken my horizon. Even though daily life was not easy, I was still standing thanks to Mam Khady, Sorano, and my big brother Fallou. Everyone was making sacrifices to help the family.

Fallou had left Kaolack before me to further his education in Dakar. He put his education on hold in 10th grade to look for a job as a gas station attendant to help our mother. This position enabled Fallou to support me financially. Out of his monthly salary of 50,000 Fcfa, he would give me 15,000 Fcfa, send some to our mother, and would juggle to live with what was left. Needless to say, money was tight.

As a PR secretary for my English club, I would often speak on behalf of the group, and would be the representative when visiting other schools. I needed to put my best foot forward and make everyone proud. But my only clothing was a pair of ragged jeans, an old shirt, and run-down sandals. I had to give speeches in that shame-inducing get-up. I mentioned this in passing to my brother Fallou, and two weeks later, on a Saturday, he took me to the Colobane market in Dakar.

At the clothing booths, he bought me five shirts, three pairs of jeans, one pair of Nike sneakers and one pair of Sébago shoes. My friends would all be surprised to see me without my usual uniform, I thought. After the market, I went to the mosque and prayed. At the end of the service, I realized that I had been too fast in thanking God for giving me new garments, because, in the mosque like everywhere else in Dakar, there were thieves. This time they had stolen my humble possessions: second-hand clothing.

This couldn't be! I thought about the expense incurred by my brother, and about the need to dress up for the next few sessions of twinning between the English clubs of the various high schools. With my friend Amadou, then a salesman in the Colobane market, we went to see a gang of young people famous for stealing and reselling merchandise. I was revolted, burning with anger, fully aware of Fallou's sacrifices for me. I couldn't let this go. Rage and fury numbed my fear to confront the thieves; I thought and felt as though I was invincible.

My friend Amadou and I tried the diplomatic approach with the gang, arguing that we were "all youngsters" to no avail. Then we used the spiritual approach with a thousand pleas. It was somewhat useful because they admitted that they were the thieves, but refused to give back any of my things. Amadou barked with anger, but it didn't help.

Even though Fallou had promised to give me more money to buy more clothing, I knew to what degree he was hurting financially and wanted to spare him additional spending. Therefore, I decided to try a supposedly very effective method: strength! Along with my cousin Pacha, known for his muscles, Amadou and I went back to the gang of thieves. Upon seeing Pacha's muscles and frown, they only admitted the theft of the Sébago shoes, which they returned. One week later, my brother bought me new clothing to save face.

In the English club, the "English Club day" was organized once a year: It was a gathering of all the clubs in the city of Dakar. The club was for me a place where to practice leadership. Every Wednesday, I would arrive home after sunset. My commitment was rewarded the following year when I was elected President of the club. I was often writing long letters to my mother and had them brought to her by cousins who had to go to Kaolack. She was encouraging me and was begging me to be cautious of the bad people, very numerous on Dakar streets. I was telling her that I had no time to socialize with people who could bring me down. My dream was elsewhere!

During 11th grade, there was a wind of happiness in my life. It materialized in a feminine presence: too brilliant a student. At first sight, I could tell that she came from a well-to-do family and that she was poised. After our first contact in the schoolyard, and our first conversations on light topics, I felt she would play a significant role in my life. With my usual eagerness, I told her the following day about my feelings, and my wish that she become my girlfriend. She raised an eyebrow in surprise. "We only spoke yesterday," she said. "Yes, but between yesterday and today, your name and the vision of you have been all over my thoughts," I answered. She smiled, half puzzled, and half won. Time was my ally, and my relationship with Fatima became what I had hoped for in the long run. She liked my ambition and my determination to move forward. Fatima was the complete opposite of me. She came from a wealthy family and lived in the beautiful neighborhood of Résidence Pointe in Dakar while I was still living in the little room at Mam Khady's in the Medina ghetto.

Fatima was special; she had appeared at a time when I needed her. We lived a pure, strong, and sincere love, although without any physical intimacy. Fatima knew my story, except for the part about my child. Everywhere in Kaolack, I was judged for fathering a child in those conditions because it was a severe thing, and nothing said that Fatima would not reject me if she learned about my son. So, I didn't tell her anything.

Since she loved me, her mother loved me unconditionally. She loved me like a son, even though Fatima's brothers were quite suspicious of this boy in tatters who was always with their sister until sunset. Fatima was pious, well bred, the kind of young woman that you don't often meet in the city of Dakar, corrupted by numerous plagues. However, we were never able to go out. In school we barely saw each other since we were not in the same grade, it was mostly at her home that we would write love poems and talk about our dreams. She was great at listening to me when I spoke about my dreams of America and my need to be militant.

At Fatima's, I had everything you can dream of in a house—comfortable armchairs, a large TV set with cable, a big fridge always filled with good things, and mostly a wonderful cook, her mom, who never hesitated preparing us tasty dishes. She knew my preference for soupoukadia. Sometimes, Fatima would buy me hamburgers at the local fast-food joint. Those were my first hamburgers. She would buy two when I visited with my friend Amadou. She had inherited this generosity from her mother. She was generous with her time, her possessions, and her thoughts for me.

Unfortunately, at the time I had nothing to offer Fatima other than my love for her and the promise to succeed yet, she believed in me and would say so. For example, to spare me a long walk, Fatima would call a taxi and pay the fare for me. It could cost up to 1500 Fcfa. A real fortune! Therefore, I would get in the cab, and as soon as Fatima was back home, I would pretend I had forgotten something, send the taxi away and take back the 1500 Fcfa. That way I could buy another hamburger, walk home, and keep the difference for more important things than a cab ride, which was too much of a luxury for a young destitute like me.

My year was turning out to be better than I initially anticipated. My relationship with Fatima had tremendously enhanced my life. I had an attentive ear and a comforting voice. I was proving to be a good president for the English club, to the point where I was reelected the following year while in Terminal (12th grade), the year of the baccalaureate. However, one event shook my fragile equilibrium. My brother Fallou, who had been supporting me, lost his job at the gas station, two months before the exam, because of the economic duress in the area.

An intense pressure began to close in on all sides. Out of the twenty-eight children in my family, I would be the first one to take the test, and maybe to pass it.

I keep a special place for Fatima in my memories. Her generosity and friendship gave me access to a world in which I was unfamiliar. Thanks to her, I got rid of my instinct to self-censor. Fatima insisted that I dare to imagine passing my baccalaureate exam and doing everything to attain that objective. She encouraged me to pursue my goals, and was a source of motivation, always pushing me to do my best. Fatima was my rock; her friendship was invaluable.

CHAPTER VII

THE TEST

"Any obstacle strengthens the determination. He who has set a goal does not change." Léonard de Vinci

The baccalaureate ("bac") exam in French-speaking countries is a national diploma that validates the completion of general secondary education.

Without the bac, the doors of universities remain closed. In the public mind, no high-ranking management career was possible, rightly so. Here, if you failed your bac, you failed in life (except for a miracle). This exam is a rite of passage; it is sacred and gives you social status by positioning you as a "youngster with a future." If you fail the exam, your parents cry, your mother falls on the ground and weeps, uncles and aunts lose sleep. As early as the first day in kindergarten, there is only one goal for the parents: the bac!

On Monday, the first day of the test, I got up at 5:00 am– neighborhood was still dark and asleep, to clean my room, say my prayers. Once at the exam center, I was surprised to notice that I was very early. There were not many of us, and the gate was still closed. A little while later the sweep of cars and motorcycles started that every year punctuated the day of that crucial exam. Parents dropping off their children with pats on their backs and last-minute advice would wait a while before leaving. Emotional and hesitant, they waited as if they were delivering their children for a gladiator fight and were not sure to see them again. Even though all this looked a little over-dramatic, it was not ridiculous. It was the bac!

About 40 minutes after my arrival, I recognized a familiar motorcycle roar: It was Pape Diop, who lived in the same house as me. "Here is your National Identity Card. You must have forgotten it when you were getting ready for your prayers," he said. How could I have forgotten the key document! Without my ID, I wouldn't have been able to enter the building and start the test. Soon after Pape Diop left, the bell rang, the doors opened, and we got down to work.

Two days after the last test, I went Fallout and Amadou to await the result. There were four times as many people as for the tests itself, since most candidates had come, like me, with their loved ones. Parents were bringing food for their children, yet we did not even have money for bread, but that was not the point. Hunger was part of our everyday life.

While we waited, we talked about Mother's situation in Kaolack. About the stormy atmosphere, she had to endure the poverty at home, and what we could do about it. Fallou—my companion in the struggle, my brother and great friend, who never judged me—said with a smile, that I would pass the exam, and that I would be the first to do so in our family. Trying to lift up my spirits he added, "You will do great, and you will be able to help Mother."

Every minute was like an eternity as we waited in line at Lycée Lamine Guéye. We waited for 11 long hours, from 8:00am to 7:00

pm. It was not extraordinary, since other candidates were waiting too, but most had eaten and we hadn't.

Around 7:00 pm, the feverish crowd started pointing in the direction of the building second floor. The principal appeared at the window, with the list of the selected candidates. The admission rate was announced: Barely 21% for this exam center: 1999 was not a good year. My candidate number was 124, and there was no 124 on the list. My forehead was sweating profusely, I felt a strange, hard to describe discomfort all over my body. Amadou and Fallou were holding my hands.

Then the principal read the list of admissible candidates who would have a chance to pass once they took the exam again. The list was very short and fit a single page. It was a great moment of solitude, even though I had friends around me. I held my breath, waiting for the very second that would seal my fate. Was I going to be a loser as my father had predicted or was I going to cross the threshold of the baccalaureate, and be allowed then to dream of America and the future?

On the second list, there was a number 124 followed by my name. I had never heard it so loud and clear. It resonated in the loudspeaker, in the presence of witnesses: I had a chance. I was not ecstatic, but relieved. My brother, my friend, and I burst into tears. We hugged, and then we sniveled like girls. We were crying with happiness, with hunger, with exhaustion. I had not passed yet, but I had not failed either; I would have to outperform myself during the oral exam to be admitted.

We visited Sorano with the news, he congratulated me and encouraged me to work hard to prepare. He then lent me a phone so that I could call my mother with the news. Usually not very expressive, she cried with joy and promised she would continue to pray. She then shared the news with my father who said, "he didn't care."

The oral test was scheduled for the following day. I dashed to study with Ousmane Sarr, a brilliant classmate who lifted my spirits and helped me study philosophy and English, the two subject matters I had to retake. Ousmane said, "you are in a better position than the others, don't waste any time thinking that you should have passed in one go. Once you pass after the retake, no-one will know whether it was in one go or not". Ousmane was truly intelligent. He had a quick mind and a never-failing memory. He accomplished his dream of going to France, became a renowned writer, and became one of the first African Scrabble champions.

Once again, the results were to be announced the day after the oral exam. Fallou, Amadou and I went back to see the list. This time, it was a sure thing, I was a bachelor. We were overwhelmed with joy, and so was Sorano. I called my mother again to share the news and listened as she recited blessings and prayers.

"These are the real diplomas in life, parents' blessings" Sorano reminded me. We celebrated my bac thanks to his generosity, and he invited us to dinner in the restaurant that had just opened near the National Theater.

Although the bac is an excellent thing to have, there is life after the bac, and I was wondering what the next step would be for me. I had to choose between a public university, Sheikh Anta Diop in Dakar, and going to the United States. Regardless of my choice, I would have to work harder than ever. My father, informed of my success, had reacted with his typical indifference and quickly clarified that he had no intention of financing my education. Friends of mine were already at the university and were often telling me about the difficult conditions in which they had to study in the public school system. Students had to sit on the floor for lack of sufficient seating in the auditorium. During class, it was often impossible to take notes because for lack of a microphone they couldn't hear the teacher. None of these things mattered. My father had proven once again that he would not support me no matter how hard the struggle or how strong the cause.

On these campuses, young people rarely completed their education without getting an ulcer, since they had difficulty buying food. The student buses were more often in the shop than on campus, forcing them to walk. The most brilliant bac graduates would get a scholarship ranging from 18 000 Fcfa–for a half-scholarship–to 32 000 Fcfa (the equivalent of 35 or 50 dollars). But in terms of proportion, the recipients of these scholarships amounted to no more than 20%. Those recipients, even though they had to juggle those meager resources, were often choosing to attend several faculties in order to stay on campus as long as possible and keep receiving the scholarship. It was a survival strategy, especially for those who also had a place to stay. It was sparing them from the harsh realities of the job market, the housing market, or the responsibilities that come with having children. They were professional students. And when the scholarship monies were late, or the food in the cafeteria was bad, there was always solidarity between pupils. They would go on strike, sometimes for a legitimate reason, but by doing so they often opened the door to spiraling out of control. They would write insults on the walls, boycott classes, block university doors, burn tires… it was chaotic and appalling. But it is a reality that is replayed day-after-day in many African countries. In spite of it all, we were often surprised that there was no better fit between the needs of the job market and the training of students. As a matter of fact, the needs of our young people were usually at the bottom of our government priorities, along with the risk of transforming the university into a temple of street-savviness and improvisation.

Between that and the unknown, the choice was clear. My dream of America possessed me. It was an inescapable expectation. America, at all costs.

At no time, did I surrender to doubt. I did question myself but did not give up on my dream. It seemed crazy to have such goals, can you imagine? However, when I considered my path from Kaolack to passing the baccalaureate exam, what I had already overcome was significant. I had done the hardest part, despite the lack of support, and even opposition from my father. I realized that I had created momentum and that my actions could change my life. I found a way to overcome what seemed to be impossible.

PART III

CHAPTER VIII

DREAM OF AMERICA

"Success is to fall seven times, stand up eight." Japanese proverb

Very few people in the world master the meaning of the verb "to leave" as well as the Senegalese people. And there is absolutely no irony in saying that emigrants are one of Senegal's main exports. Strong and ambitious, either dreamers or completely deluded, they launch into adventure and bet everything they own on the one and only number they think lucky: immigration. Just like in any betting game, most lose, and the lucky ones win. First by landing in their dreamland, then by making enough money to send back home.

Most of the time, the young people who decide to leave have a motto "Barçaou barsakh": the first word is the abbreviation of the Spanish town of Barcelona, which for a while was one of the preferred destinations of illegal emigrants from Senegal; and the second term means "hell" in the Senagalese language Wolof. In other words, there is but one alternative: leaving or a living hell. This "choice" makes full sense when you consider that the one who leaves does not only leave for his own sake. The importance of his mission is ingrained from a tender age. It is an assignment for the boy, who is de facto designated as the person in charge of his family's well-being. He is the one who will go seek a better future for the sake of his loved ones. The one who will go get a real opportunity and a chance to be happy. It is not really a choice, but rather a silent obligation and a heavy responsibility for a young man. Over time, this responsibility is more and more burdensome, scary, pressing. Young men leave for their father, their mother, their brothers, and their sisters. They leave out of duty, out of the desire to be of service, out of the need to contribute to the family happiness. This is why some of them, blinded by the promise of a better tomorrow, die before they reach their destination. They do not measure the risks and so leave on a canoe, in the baggage hold of a plane, hidden behind a car bumper. The means of transportation doesn't matter much, the goal is to leave. Leave to never come back. Leave at all costs, because there is no other option. They leave, betting big, and trust the saying that goes: "The higher the risk, the greater and better the outcome."

Social segmentation is very palpable when you leave Dakar to go to villages like Thiès, Ziguinchor or Kaolack, where I come from. This phenomenon is typical of urbanization in many countries of the world.

In Senegal, there are three options for young people.

First option: to be those who leave the country and sacrifice, knowing well that they have everything to lose and everything to win. Sometimes they get lucky, but sometimes not, unfortunately.

Second option: to be those who decide to stay and fight, hoping to make it one day. In that group, you find many cases of success due only to hard work, which belies those of us who always thought that leaving was the only way to success. Maybe they have more to lose. Maybe they have a wider and stronger support base. Regardless of their decision, it stems more from differences in social and economic conditions than from courage. This is due to our self-image, to our view of our condition, and to our determination.

Third option: to be those who stay to prepare tea all day, without any concern for more fulfilling tasks. They drop out of school very early, and no speech on the value of working can reach them. However, they are unsurpassable at brewing good ataya . And they can stay idle all day without any concern for the growing stack of bills, because they know that those who have left to go abroad will send money to take care of everything.

At the time when I asked myself the ultimate question, whether to stay or to go. I already knew the answer. In my family, I wasn't the only one. My brother Fallou was doing all he could to go to Italy. He had already made up his mind. He had started the immigration procedures and had gotten his visa. His departure was certain and imminent. We had the same goal: leave for a better future. By being two, we could double our chances of succeeding. We were, one more time, linked by the mission of protecting our family's well-being. We were a united team, bonding over our old friendship, and above all by a burning desire to change the course of our lives.

One thing was truly implacable: Fallou's fast-approaching departure. His path was as carefully planned as mine was unclear. I had asked him to take me to seek advice from an older boy from Kaolack who had spent time in the United States. He was staying in Dakar's best hotel. The place was so beautiful that we felt completely out of place. Everything was new and shiny. The first thing that struck us was the air conditioning. The cool air provided an indescribable feeling of relief. It was a positive omen, hinting that immigrating to the United States was going to be a successful endeavor.

I was curious and excited, and my eyes were scanning the place, up, down, left, right, at an incredible speed. We went to the front desk to announce ourselves. The staff was courteous and welcoming in spite of our shabby clothing, far removed from the dress code of their usual guests. We didn't mind. We had the nobility of humility, the strength of our will, the wealth of our hope. Fallou was on his way to Italy, and I was on my way to the United States.

We had to go up to the eighth floor, suite number eighty-four. We were told to use the elevator next to the lobby. It was our first time in that strange machine, exhilarating and fun. A little bell had rung, the doors had opened and closed after us. I pressed the number eight button, the bell rang again and we started ascending. I was thinking of the symbol, the hidden message in this climb. Fallou was not as enthusiastic. After all, he was only escorting me. I was about to share my thoughts with him when the elevator stopped. We both grew very concerned, staring at each other without saying a word. We stopped breathing, hoping maybe to become lighter.

Fallou reminded me of the hesitation he had had before following me. He swore he had felt a bad vibe upon getting in that elevator. He forgot that he was the older one of us and accused me mercilessly. "If we die here, and I don't go to Italy, it will be all your fault. It will weigh on your conscience."

"But if we die here, I will no longer have a conscience," I said, amused.

Fallou didn't appreciate the joke, and couldn't understand my humor in spite of the elevator breakdown. I could sense his tears—or rather his sweat as he describes it today. He was already envisioning the end of his future in Italy. But, as he started rambling about regrets and accusations, the strange machine resumed its course, and we started laughing.

Safely out of our small cell, we were greeted by our host. The meeting was short and useful, not necessarily in terms of details and actual advice, but more importantly because his experience confirmed my decision. I was going to leave for the United States with a bit more light. This man was living proof that leaving rhymes with returning, with comfort, with reassurance, with homecoming, and with a better life. I would leave and also return to Senegal. I would leave to explore my capabilities, and I would leave the United States to come back. That is what I told myself.

Every night, I was sleeping with America at my bedside. This great country, symbolized by a photo of the Statue of Liberty cut out from a magazine, was in my thoughts and in my dreams. I liked everything about the American way of life: fast food, hip-hop, RnB, the whims of the Hollywood stars. I liked it all. I loved the freedom, the greatness, the feeling that everything was possible. I believed in the idea conveyed in the media that America was the world's pinnacle of excellence, because Americans like a challenge. It made me want to go even more. My understanding of the world was in sync with what the United States stood for.

"When the going gets tough, the tough gets going," said John Fitzgerald Kennedy.

Along with my education, I was actively preparing the paperwork that would allow me to land in Uncle Sam's territory. It was at the end of my year in seconde (tenth grade) that I had made my decision. I had visited the embassy, where they were surprised that I didn't even know that a passport was required to travel. Back then, getting a passport cost fifteen thousand francs CFA (approximately thirty dollars). This was a huge amount of money for me. It was during the summer holiday and if I wanted a passport, there was only one-way: I had to get a job.

The following day, I applied for any job and every job. I filled out job applications in restaurants, in bars, in clothing stores, in supermarkets. There are things that you can find easily in Dakar, but a job is not one of them. I had to call on my young uncle, Pape Diop, who was an architect and working on a construction site. He brainstormed with me, but to no avail. I then suggested I could become a worker on his construction site. He was strongly opposed to it, explaining that I had no skills in that area, and that I would be doing physically challenging tasks. "This job would be too difficult for someone with a light build like you," he said. I insisted every morning before he would leave for work and every night at the dinner table. This harassment lasted fifteen long days. I was getting better at tricking him and his defenses were weakening. He finally gave in and introduced me to the manager of the construction site of the Arts Village in Dakar, financed by the Ministry of Culture. The workers' boss, a young man with biceps as large as tree trunks, with a face and body all white from the cement dust, asked my name. "Thione," I said. "I am Pape Diop's nephew." He said without kidding that he was the boss. He pointed out that there was no cousin or nephew on his site, that he could see that I was skinny, and that I would get no special treatment so as to not upset the other workers.

"Work starts at eight a.m., which doesn't mean "eight oh one," and finishes at seven p.m.—but that is a movable time. Seven p.m. can be seven thirty or even seven forty-five. There is a one-hour break at midday for those who bring food. If you don't bring anything, you will simply work through the break. If you are lazy, I will fire you. I have already fired many people."

After this introduction, he ordered me to dig a trench with a hache. I had just turned seventeen, and I was not going to spend my vacation idly. I had often heard grown-ups say that life is hard: I thought I knew what it meant, but I was entirely wrong. This boss was honing my education and my understanding of the concept of hardship in life.

I was surprised by the toughness of the work. I was just like a slave. That too was reminding me of America and of the slave trade.

Before this experience as a worker, I knew that one can sleep from tiredness, but I didn't know that one can also lose sleep from too much tiredness. I was walking five miles every day, was eating only at night, and was constantly in pain. My pain was so intense that I couldn't sleep. It was impossible to lie down in a comfortable position. All my muscles were sore, even the ones I didn't know I had.

However, I was getting used to my job. From the mason apprentices whom I had always thought to be intellectually limited, I learned a lot, on a lot of topics. We would talk politics, philosophy, and travel, sometimes while eating peanuts. I met very intelligent people who I worked with from Monday to Saturday. On Sunday, I would pray and read. In these people lay a treasure: a trove of experiences, advice and lessons that I had been stupid enough to bury under a thick layer of stereotypes and ignorance.

On the twenty-eighth day my body gave up. Back home after a long day of work, I spent the night throwing up. Handling the spade on an empty stomach, under Dakar's punishing sun and without any sleep, had floored me. I had not been able to recuperate, which had a brutal effect on my entire being. The first reaction was to self-medicate, so my uncles and aunts gave me acetaminophen, to no effect. I was then taken to the Dantec hospital, by my uncle who paid 5,000 FCFA, or $10, for a doctor consultation. The doctor simply prescribed some rest and prohibited me from returning to work.

I was only two days away from payday. Two days! With the boss being uncompromising, I was wondering about my fate after twenty-eight days instead of the planned thirty. Two days later, I was very surprised when Pape Diop brought me my salary, 28,000 FCFA. It was the equivalent of twenty-eight days each paid 1,000 FCFA, or $2. I was moved, proud, and filled with joy and hope. The pressure vanished. I was finally able to relax, and at last to fall asleep.

My salary enabled me to pay the stamp for the passport (15,000 FCFA, or $25), to take pictures for 2,000 FCFA ($4). I sent 5,000 FCFA ($10) to my mother and kept the remaining 6,000 FCFA ($10 or so), for the various costs of the passport. I was very proud to have bought this document with my own sweat. I had bought the right to materialize my dream, I was no longer living in abstraction. I was creating the means to live out my destiny.

My knowledge of the American educational system was somewhat sketchy. All I knew was that university in America were prohibitively expensive. My dream sometimes seemed pretentious, but not unattainable. How would I pay for an education in an American university when I couldn't even afford to eat twice a day? In my search for reasonably priced colleges, a friend of Pape Diop called Jean-Paul recommended Cuyahoga Community College. The process for applying was different from that of traditional universities: Normally, I should have passed the TOEFL (Test Of English as a Foreign Language) before being admitted. It would have cost me $100, or 50,000 FCFA, to take the exam. Since I had no budget for this (or for anything else, for that matter) I chose the solution of doing a prep year upon my arrival, in order to speak English well enough for my university education.

Cuyahoga Community College replied quickly after I requested a pre-admission application by mail. I received a thick package, which filled me with enthusiasm— school transcripts, letters of recommendation; I piled up all my academic wealth and filled out the forms to quickly send in my full application. I got a pre-admission without too much difficulty, but another, even more decisive obstacle was coming my way.

High achievers recognize that regularly evaluating and breaking down goals into steps facilitates progress. My acceptance at the Cuyahoga Community College was already a wonderful victory, but choosing to do a prerequisite year on arrival required that I manage covering my personal finances while immersing myself in school and mastering American English. I had to master the language in order to excel in my university studies, and to immerse myself in the American culture. To this day, I strive to concentrate on one key objective at a time, so as not to spread myself too thin and dampen my spirits. If the circumstances allow, take one step at a time.

CHAPTER IX

DEDICATION RHYMES
WITH EXPECTATION

"Examine If what you promise is right and possible, for the promise is a debt." Confucius

To move one step forward in the direction of my dream, I had to prove my ability to support the cost of my education. My bank statement had to show a balance of $14,000 or 7 million FCFA. Of course I didn't have the money. A friend of Mam Khady's wrote a letter of financial support for me, stating that he was the tutor for my education. From there, I could easily apply for a visa.

At dawn one day, I went to the Embassy of the United States. My friend Amadou came along. The embassy doors would not open before 9 a.m., but everybody knows that in order to get the visa one must get up early to be among the first people in the waiting line. That day, all the visa hopefuls had had the same idea: at six in the morning, the line was already a long serpentine. Incredible! One could fell the stress in each other's eyes. The atmosphere was tense. Each one of us was praying silently for God to help us in getting the visa, the key to the land of freedom. At nine o'clock, the embassy doors opened and we came in quietly, cautiously, as if afraid of shattering our dream.

Teller number two gestured for me to approach her. She was a young Asian woman, whose face I will never forget. She asked for my supporting documents, looked through them quickly, and told me I didn't have enough. "You need fourteen thousand dollars. There is only seven thousand in your account." Naïvely, I tried to soften her up by negotiating in English. "My sister…"

She cut me short, "I am not your sister! Don't call me that. Plus, you didn't even take the BAC exam. That's it! It's over!" It was a brutal, icy shower.

Upon seeing my face, Amadou guessed that the visa had been denied. Tonton Sorano reminded me that I had another year and a half to go before the BAC. Eight months after my first rejection, I applied again with a similar result.

The famous saying, "All things come in threes" turned out to be true for me. Since the date of my college preregistration was old compared to the date of my visa request, I was asked a third time to provide a new letter from the school. It took a while for Cuyahoga to send me a new preregistration letter. For my fourth visa application, I was already a regular at the embassy. The fourth time, I had passed the BAC and almost all of my friends' classes had started at the Sheikh Anta Diop University in Dakar.

I returned to the embassy for the verdict on my fourth trial. I was praying not to meet the Asian lady who had already twice had the pleasure of stamping Denial on my passport. On January 18, 2000, teller number four called me over. I was tired. I had hung on to my dream for three long years, without making any progress. I had no more energy or resources to pursue things further. The

91

hope of better days was slipping away. I had never allowed myself to doubt, lose faith or question my abilities, or the high hopes that Mam Thione had placed in me. But at that moment, I felt that my fragile dream might be severely damaged.

He was an old man and the whiteness of his beard was immediately reassuring. As soon as he touched my documents, I felt the need to supplement my case with a spoken plea. I told him, with tears in my eyes, a heavy heart and lots of hope, that I just wanted the opportunity to get a good education in the United States in order to grow and help the mother I loved so much. Without looking up he said, "Why Cleveland? I am from Florida. It gets cold over there." He took his time to review the various documents. He finally stopped, smiled and said, "You will get your chance. Promise me that once over there you will behave and you will work hard."

"I will, I will be irreproachable and a good student," I answered in English.

He asked me to pick up my passport at 4 p.m. I did not believe him because I had already been rejected three times. I had been denied every time. Without my visa, I couldn't dream, hope or even breathe. Those who had received the same instruction in the morning, came back in the afternoon. In the morning, we were approximately one hundred. At 4 p.m. we were only twenty, and I was fourth in line. The atmosphere was more relaxed. We were talking and laughing. I didn't know why I was still apprehensive. Gone mad maybe, I started asking everyone if they had been instructed to come back for the visa. The person ahead of me in line explained that if I was asked back, it was because the visa was granted. He then asked me to calm down.

The policeman who was returning the passports handed mine with one word, "Congratulations." I had a three-year student visa— the light at the end of the tunnel.

It was like overcoming a painful and horrible fever—a fever that had lasted three years. The temperature, initially low, had risen to an alarming level. I was feeling weak, exhausted. I had worked with all my soul, all my strength to fight the fever, to nip it, because at a certain degree it makes you delirious. Because of this fever, many had lost their minds, and had not been able to go further. Now the fever was gone, and my honor, my dreams and my hopes were intact. I had my visa. At last! I had the key to my future.

Fatima reminded me that the United Sates would be fertile grounds for developing my activism. A few months earlier, she had witnessed how the death of a twenty-three-year-old man called Amadou Diallo had angered me. Amadou was living in the US, among the Peul community in New York City. He had been shot on the evening of February 4, 1999, near his apartment building, by four policemen of the NYC Street Crime Unit. There were nineteen bullets in his body, and he was not even armed. I had said that if I had been in the States at the time, I would have marched to condemn this kind of abuse.

I was ignorant of what was behind the gate separating America from the rest of the world. How many surprises would there be for me? The euphoria of getting the visa was too intense to dwell on the thousand questions I had about the United States. So I left the embassy and rushed to Tonton Sorano to bring him the news. The hug that followed was heartwarming. From his office, as usual, I called my parents' neighbor in Kaolack, to speak to my mother. (Because we didn't have a phone at home, I would call the neighbors who in turn would call my mother.) But this time there was no waiting, because she had already been waiting at the neighbors' for over an hour, anxious to know the outcome of my fourth application. Her happiness was beyond words when she learned I had gotten the visa.

However, when the great joy receded, she asked me how we would buy the plane ticket for the trip from Dakar and New York. The lowest price was roughly $1,000 (approximately 500,000 FCFA).

The day before obtaining the visa, I had had an intuitive feeling that almost felt like an order. I had to visit Oumou Salamata Niass, daughter of the Sheikh. I had to go get her blessing. She was one of the few people who knew about my project, and that day she asked where I was going to stay in New York. When I answered that I didn't know anyone in the United States, she informed me that her husband lived there and promised that he, a taxicab driver in New York, could pick me up at the airport, and even better, host me until I could find longer-term arrangements. That promise had soothed me, but the plane ticket problem remained.

My mother went to ask a loan from all the people she knew who were supposedly wealthy: merchants, marabous, inheritors in Dakar as well as in Kaolack. Hostility was the only response she got, although we kept showing the title of my grandfather's house as a guarantee for the loan. Time was fleeting. It had already been five months since I had gotten the visa and I was still roaming Dakar, for lack of a plane ticket. I got to the point where I could only wait for a miracle. My mother said it didn't seem like me. But I was very discouraged, and I believed I had to accept my fate.

Mommy offered me to go visit Daouda, a distant cousin who had made it in Japan and was visiting Senegal. "Like all the others he will take the time to really listen to our problems and will then explain why he can't help us and once we are gone he will make fun of our destitution." My answer did not sway my mother's optimism. It is universally known that mothers always have treasures of energy, faith, and fighting spirit for their children, even when they are desperate. That is what made the difference. She had taken up the challenge for me. Begging every day was more draining and exhausting than the job I'd had as a construction worker. My pain was endless, my despair infinite.

After her meeting with her cousin Daouda, my mother called me to announce that he wanted to meet with me at the Mboup travel agency in Dakar. He granted me a loan for buying the ticket. The date was May 19, 2000. He asked when I wanted to leave. "As soon as possible," I said impatiently. So he bought me a ticket on the next flight to New York. He took dollars out of his wallet to pay. It was the first time I was seeing this currency, the object of so much fantasizing. The bills were all the same size, the same color, probably the same scent. They gave him his change of $20, which he handed to me with gravitas. I thanked him profusely, promising that once in America, my priority would be to work in order to pay him back as quickly as possible.

I told Oumou Salamata Niass of my departure date and received her blessings. She kept her husband informed of my planned arrival. My friend Amadou had said I should not forget that it gets cold in the US. He recommended, rather imperatively, that I buy a raincoat. "That's what people wear over there to protect against the cold."

"No, I don't think so," I said. A little debate ensued, but it was hard to debate with Amadou. I gave in, a bit puzzled that Americans would don, to fight the cold, what the Senegalese wear when it rains, or what the Senegalese fishermen wear on their boats. We left to buy a raincoat at the second-hand clothing market in Colobane. For that very special day, I should wear a suit, I had told myself. We found a good used one, at a good price, and also a used raincoat, which was not really the right size for me—but I was happy. The suit was as wellfitting as if it had been custom-made. It was blue, striped, with four buttons. It was the first time I was wearing a suit of my own. Previously, I had only dressed up for the occasional event at the English club. I would borrow a jacket from my uncle and pants from my brother Fallou, but both men were taller than me.

During this period of my life, I seized opportunities and accepted help from others, while remaining diligent, focused and persistent. I consciously put forth my best effort, and worked to remain level-headed despite my increased responsibilities within the community. Conscientious service to others was something that highly impacted me, proved to be an invaluable tool, and a source of motivation.

CHAPTER X

AMERICA, HERE I COME

"No stone can not be polished without friction, no man can perfect his experiment without a test." Confucius

It was D-day. Oddly, Ousseynou was in Dakar, available to help me pack. We were in the Mbop neighborhood, in Fallou's small apartment where I lived since he had moved to Italy. I went to see Tonton Sorano. I was expecting to see him half-sad, half-happy, but no! The man with special energy was euphoric. He was elated to see me go and fulfill my dreams.

Then I went to see Fatima to say good-bye, and to kiss her mother who had been, for many months, like a sweet mother to me. I had often heard that long-distance relationships were doomed to fail, that couples separate. We were not even at that level of commitment yet, but Fatima promised that she would wait for me for as long as needed. I knew her to be faithful and trustworthy. Although we had said good-bye, Fatima came to my place, a bittersweet surprise that gave me the feeling that I counted a lot for her. The idea that

I was leaving Fatima for at least three years was certainly damping the mood.

At night, April 24, 2000, dressed in my (unbeknownst to me) ridiculous attire, we took a taxi at 10:45 p.m. for a flight departing at 3:45 a.m. I took a last look at my surroundings. In the cab, Ousseynou and Amadou were discussing flight duration, weather forecast, and various other mundane topics, mostly to fill the silence. I was passively contributing to this conversation through simple, monosyllabic answers.

"No" and "Ah, yes!"

My thoughts were elsewhere. When the house was about to disappear in the dark distance, I turned around and looked at the roof. That same roof on which Fallou and I had reinvented the world; the roof from which we were staring at the low-flying planes, not believing that one day we would be inside one of those machines.

That night, it was my turn. I was about to live my dream of going to America. But mostly, I was going to get a career in order to care for my mother and my son, and to help Anta herself get a future. I had not been able to see my mother before leaving and that was making me very sad. She was at home in Kaolack. And after the last hurdle to get a loan for the plane ticket, another trip to Dakar for my mother would have been too much for the family. I was thinking about her face, her eyes in which I had found the ultimate strength for my journey. I was thinking of the motherly gestures she would have had on the way to the taxi, and of her words: the last blessings, the last bits of advice. I wanted to tell her about everything: my fright, my angst, and my doubts. But luckily, I was able to talk to her on the phone. My feelings were mixed. So instead of talking, I decided to listen to her. She said a prayer for me, blessed me, and then was silent. Our time was up, every minute was depleting my meager phone credit. "Mother!" I called. "Mother? Are you there?" I didn't hear the tone indicating the end of the call, so I knew she was still at the other end; but why was she not speaking? I heard a sob. My mother's vocal chords had been silenced by the sadness of seeing me go. Like any mother, she was fighting to hide her sorrow, but she was shedding tears of worry and tears of pride and joy. Just when I started reassuring her, the call was over. I had no more money to call back. I had lost her. My heart was heavy, my mind confused. I was angry about not having been able to properly say good-bye. Angry for not having said, "See you soon, Mother." Angry for not having said, "Thank you. Thank you for everything."

I channeled this energy into my drive to succeed. Going back to the past and wondering endlessly was not my style. I would move forward, for my mother, for my family, to honor Mam Thione's memory. I lowered my head, put my hands on my chest, closed my eyes and focused on my mission and the moment.

Once at the airport, I said my goodbyes to my companions of struggle, Amadou and Ousseynou. They were sad to see me go, and I saw that in their walk and in their posture, even though they were trying to hide it. They couldn't go any farther, because they had no plane ticket. Our paths were separating. We had been together for better and for worse, and now my companions, my brothers were no longer going to be with me for my new challenge. I was going to be by myself, all by myself.

Although Ousseynou and Amadou were the only ones there with me, I was thinking about all the people whose care had brought me to that airport terminal. The wisdom of Mam Thione, the unconditional love of my mother, the attentions of Fallou, the gentleness of Fatima, the support of Ousseynou, the never-wavering encouragements of Tonton Sorano, the valiant masons, Mam Khady, Pape Diop, Madame Lawson, and the English club. So many faces, lessons, proofs of love, and faith in me. I also thought of all the people who had made my life difficult, he indifference and hate of my father. I thought of all the hurdles that I'd had to endure—my roving days without a high school, the French Cultural Center, the Dakar gang, and my record high number of rejections at the US embassy. All these challenges had tested my determination, my faith, my will, and my humility—and they had prepared me. Good and bad times had shaped me and made me what I was, what I thought, what I believed in, what I respected, and what I would become.

As I was walking into the belly of the airport, I could still feel the presence of my old world, which I was about to leave. I had only one light bag in hand, because I didn't own much. However, I was probably the person most burdened in terms of baggage. Emotions, advice, prayers, blessings—I was ready.

Through the glass walls, I could still see Ousseynou and Amadou. They kept me in their sights until the last second, and waved a huge good-bye. This meant, "Go conquer the United States, go fulfill your dreams and those that you carry for us. Don't worry about us, we'll do fine. Go for it!"

I answered their wave, moved and teary. I started slowly walking backwards to show my respect. Respect for their friendship, for the loyalty between us. They were them, and I was me. Now, they were no more. I could no longer see them. I went through the check-in, wondering if this was not yet another dream. With the boarding pass in hand, I thought about my friends. How would they get home? Would they have food for dinner that evening? Although my future in the US was far from certain, I knew that I would eat that night. Our paths had separated, already our fates were different. Not better, not opposed, only different.

When I boarded the plane, my heart started beating like mad. It was a strange feeling, a mix of excitement and apprehension. I was flying for the first time in my life. The company was Air Afrique. I was wondering how many people would be on the plane, where the luggage was going, and how we would sleep in seats so close to one another. I also noticed the flight attendants' uniforms. The staff was entirely African, from various parts of the continent. They were all smiling, speaking fluently in several languages. I wondered what kind of education they'd had, and if the ladies' shoes were comfortable.

My train of thought suddenly stopped with an intriguing question. I wondered what the restrooms were like. Aloof and completely ignorant, I stood up although the security signs were on. A lady attendant asked me to return to my seat. Once I was finally able to visit the restrooms, I was amazed by what I saw. I had never used a Western toilet, except at my girlfriend Fatima's. I stayed there for twenty minutes, standing up and staring at everything, trying to solve a mystery—the destination of what the passengers leave in the restrooms. Like any good African, I couldn't help but think, "Whites are something."

My takeaway from this journey: accept the range of emotions that you experience when a huge event occurs in your life, like my eagerly awaited flight to the USA. Your memories and experiences are invaluable and will always have an impact on you. Acknowledge the positive aspects of every situation and remain optimistic.

In new experiences do not allow yourself to succumb to fear. When you do not know something, say so, and don't be afraid to ask questions. Being sincere is always the best solution.

CHAPTER XI

TWENTY DOLLARS IN MY POCKET

"Your dreams require you to risk, to abandon the comfort, to exist in the world to be different, disturbing, and to believe in you." M-C Turgeon

I didn't shut my eyes during the flight. I had to be the witness of my dream. My journey started with an observation phase. I tried to imprint everything onto my mind: the exit doors, the light displays, the safety belts, and the numerous buttons on the back of the seat in front of me. Before take-off, there was an announcement: "Welcome aboard this Air Africa flight…" The stewardess showed how to fasten the safety belts. She then continued with a somewhat terrifying explanation of the evacuation procedures in case of a crash: oxygen masks, lifejackets—where were mine?

"Maybe I should practice?" I asked the stewardess who smiled at me and assured me it was not necessary. No other passenger had made that request, so I tried to relax, which was quite difficult because of the worried excitement that I felt at listening to all the sounds around. The worse of all was a baby, wailing non-stop.

I knew that this flight was going to be long—eight long hours would eventually be between my homeland and me. During take-off, I tried to look out of the window, which was not easy because I was seating between two cumbersome men—one with his bags, the other one with his newspaper. As we were slowly rising in altitude, I managed to catch a glimpse of Dakar with its tiny lights here and there. I thought, as the airliner disappeared into low clouds, that I was leaving Kaolack, my capital, my continent. I was leaving my mother, my family, my friends, all the ones I loved. I was leaving my culture, my traditions, my habits, my climate, I was leaving all that I knew, my language, my spirituality. All that for an unknown destination in search of a future and of happiness. I was also realizing that I was leaving my dream, since I was actually living it. I had left it in terminal B, gate 2, when I boarded the plane. Now that I was sitting in the plane, with my baccalaureate diploma and a passport adorned with a visa for America, I had to reinvent a new dream! I had to push the envelope even further, dream big, in colors, in high-def! This was terrifying because I didn't have a specific goal yet. I had no clue about what was yet to come. I did not even know how I was going to eat or if I would find shelter. I had to center myself, to regenerate.

I could smell a delicious scent wafting through the entire plane, which made me happy because I hadn't had any time to eat that day. A couple of stewardesses pushing a heavy cart loaded with drinks and probably our dinner stopped at the front of the cabin and then proceeded along the aisle, in a backward direction, almost chanting, "Chicken or pasta? Anything to drink? Good evening! Chicken or pasta? Would you like bread with your dinner?" Gradually, their voices and the smells of the warm meal they were announcing intensified, enveloping me. Dinner was served! I was fully ready when the stewardess, a bit disheveled, leaned in my direction to ask what I wanted. I didn't give her time to recite the entire sentence. She had barely started, "Chicken or…" before I interrupted, "Chicken please. And some orange juice. And I will have bread. Thank you."

My food arrived piping hot, the aluminum lid keeping it warm. I looked at the passenger sitting next to me. I was not used to utilizing a fork and a knife, because in the culture where I was from, we ate with our hands. There is a whole etiquette for eating with your fingers that I could have applied there, but I did my best to imitate my neighbor. So I took the fork in my left hand and the knife in the other hand, and first worked on the meat. The plastic knife was not sharp enough, or maybe I was not very good at it. In any case, it was a disaster. I ate a few potatoes, waiting for my neighbor to focus on his tray. I had the feeling he was observing what I was doing, what I was eating and how I was doing. The neighbor on the left was already finished and was wiping his mouth contentedly. His elbow was constantly bumping my arm, interrupting my pathetic attempts at eating in a "civilized" manner. I was exasperated and hungry and I thought that using "tools" to eat was not better, and was not improving the food at all. The taste of my food remained the same, as did its texture, and I thought to myself while clumsily trying to use it, that all this artillery was only diminishing the pleasure of tasting, the pleasure of touching the food, of feeling its warmth, knowing its shape, and of being directly in contact with it.

So, in a quick motion that showed both my hunger and my decision, I threw my flatware down and started eating in the Senegalese age-old tradition.

Contented, I was finally able to think of the entertainment offered by the airline. Unfortunately, the movie had already started, and I realized that the lights had been dimmed. The flight attendants had taken away almost all the trays and some passengers were already sleeping. Me? I was too excited to sleep. Stretching would have been nice, but I didn't dare stand up for fear of waking my neighbors.

The center seat was the worst in that plane. I was unable to move one way or another. I was in the middle, like between Senegal and the US, or between my past and my future.

As the plane approached New York, I became overwhelmed with fear. The apprehension hovering over my arrival had increased. All was uncertainty.

When the captain announced that the plane would start descending towards New York City, I saw through the windows the greatness and splendor of that city, perfected by the light of dawn, landing at 8 a.m. local time, at the John Fitzgerald Kennedy airport! The shock I experienced on leaving the plane was immediate when we all had to line up for the various formalities. There was a distinction between Americans and foreigners. Above the "locals" line, a sign said, "Welcome home" and above the foreigners' line, another sign said, "Welcome to the United States". This valorization of the nationals made me think about the attitude towards citizens in our countries. Almost all over Africa, there remains a cult of the white man, and Westerners are treated like kings at the expense of the country sons. America was showing the right example.

After this little sociological comparison between my and this new country, I felt fearful. Fearful of being sent back to Senegal, which sometimes happens. I asked the closest traveler what the odds were of being denied entry. He didn't know, but he quizzed me on something else.

"Can you write?" he asked. "Okay, great—fill out this immigration form for me? It will help me, and you will forget about your stress. Pretending to be interested in me, he asked, "Have you ever been here?"

"No, or I wouldn't be so worried," I replied.

"It's okay, we'll pray together to not be rejected."

Once I arrived the immigration officer, I gave him my passport, along with my pre-registration from the university. Having noticed that no other passenger was wearing a raincoat like mine, I had taken it off and shoved it under my arm. The officer looked at the coat, then stared at me. His gaze was interrogating. He asked about my destination in Cleveland, about the reason for my presence in the USA. He finally smiled and said, "Welcome to America," then stamped my passport. My three-year visa had just been confirmed. I followed the other passengers to get my luggage. Serigne Aliou, grand-son of my spiritual guide, had traveled on the same flight. So together we got our bags back and exited together to meet Ass Dieng, son-in-law of the spiritual guide, who was going to host me. He was there, at the ready, along with Serigne Aliou's older brother. I had recognized the brother thanks to his typically Senegalese outfit: a caftan, a hat, and on his face the traits of Sheikh Ibrahima Niass whom I knew very well. Ass Dieng was a tall, good-looking man. They both reassured me: "You don't know us but we know you. Your father was our teacher at the primary school in Kaolack. That man knew how to use a horsewhip."

Hearing them talk about my father comforted me—I was with my people. They took my luggage and I followed them to the parking lot. For the first time, I was breathing American air. I exhaled. At last, America I was twenty-two years old, and starving for success.

I was expecting to see skyscrapers and monuments because that was my only obsession, but they explained that this kind of real estate does not exist near the airport.

We got on the highway to go to the Bronx. On the road, I noticed trashcans and run-down buildings, and even after forty minutes, still no skyscraper. This part of town was not the America of my imagination. I was extremely disappointed.

Once we arrived in the building where Ass Dieng lived, we saw only young blacks and Latinos young people who seemed idle, disenchanted. There was not an ounce of chic; it was the Bronx. Ass Dieng's building walls were dirty; hallways were poorly lit; everything seemed small. I was feeling a little bit like in Dakar. We waited for the elevator for almost fifteen minutes! And it arrived in a sinister cacophony. Ass was living in a modest, two-bedroom apartment, decorated with posters of Senegalese movies. He immediately tried to put us at ease, saying that I was his young brother and that as such, I had to make myself at home.

It was the wee hours of the morning, and I knew that my mother had probably not slept. I knew she would only be relieved once I would call her to say that I had made it safely, and was in good hands. Therefore, I was dying to talk to her, to tell her how everything went. The plane, the city, the trip... Ass took me to a small Pakistani store to buy a calling card. There were young people playing the music I was hearing in the American artists clip. The calling card was $10. I felt in my pocket the $20 bill that Daouda had given me. My only bill, all my wealth. In return the storekeeper gave me back $10.

It was when I took this change that I started panicking, thinking about what was going to happen. The serious things were about to start.

With my card, I went back to Ass's apartment, where I tried my best to find some privacy in a little corner. I dialed the number, with the phone tightly against my ear so as not to lose a bite of the conversation. They had me wait for a while, and went to fetch my mother. It was my first day in America, and on April 25, 2000, I had a brief, rich, and moving conversation with my mother.

She wanted to know if I was well. A question I could not answer. How can a youngster, thousands of miles away from home for the first time, with $10 in his pocket and no prospect for the future, be well? "Yes, everything is good, Maman." I knew my answer was not reassuring, because I was not confident myself and she could interpret even the tone of my voice. My anxiety was too strong for her not to notice. I was not convincing but my answer remained the same, "Everything is good." Then I called Tonton Sorano, Fatima, and Amadou who unfortunately encountered the sad truth: a flat tone indicating the end of my credit.

The promise I'd made to my mother, that as soon as I would start working she would long for nothing, was echoing in my mind. As I hung up the phone, I asked Ass what I could do to find a job. He reassured me and said that if I were not too demanding, I would be able to find something. He knew an Indian man who owned a small butcher shop.

When it was time to get settled, I met one of the first challenges of my new world: a shower! What a fantastic thing that was! What comfort! I got in, pulled the curtain after me. In the shower, there was a blue faucet and a red one. "Of these two, which should I turn?" I tried to reason. The blue one seemed basic, while the red one conveyed modernity. But the blue—no! Red is a much more exciting color." After five minutes of internal debate, I chose the red one and fully opened it. I was strategically positioned, exactly under the shower head, to enjoy the pleasure of a good shower. A relaxing shower after my long rip! The water was instantly warm and pleasant; I closed my eyes, enjoying this rain that reminded me of the torrential downpours in Dakar in the summer. But suddenly the water became hot, very hot. I leaped out of the shower. Rubbing my arm to ease the pain I was very surprised to watch the smoldering water, and realized I had just avoided a second or even third degree burn! Why such hot water? Nonsense!

Ass Dieng was very surprised to hear me say it was my first shower ever, and that I didn't know how to work it. I didn't care—the most important thing was that I had survived the ordeal. I had to find money urgently and I set out to visit the Indian butcher right away. He asked me to come back the following day. I decided to take a walk, looking for a clue to the America I was looking for. The America that had attracted me, the America I had dreamed of. Because up until then, only the ever-present English was a proof that I was in the United States.

I hadn't seen a single skyscraper yet, I was in a ghetto like the Medina in Dakar, I could see homeless people everywhere, a bit like the young street beggars in Dakar; I used to walk miles and miles in Dakar and now in New York, I was still walking. I was an apprentice in masonry in Dakar, and here I was going to work in a meat shop.

I walked while rehashing this increasing disillusion. I stopped in a pizzeria to buy some food. It was for breakfast that I decided to talk to the employee, a man with a fast talk and an incomprehensible accent. And to add insult to injury, he could not understand my accent either. My accent. Mine. Me, the president of the English club in Blaise Diagne High School in Dakar—so, to avoid being misunderstood he raised nine fingers in my direction, showing "Nine dollars. Nine!" Now, I had in hand a slice of hot pizza, a Coke, a paper napkin, and a whole dollar. I could not forget that I had the university to pay, an apartment to rent, food to buy, travels to buy, clothing—the five months between the start of my classes at college and now were my deferment. But I was not discouraged. I hadn't come that far to be so easily discouraged. This was time for action at last. Dreaming was a thing of the past. So I started work the following day and started my new career with a warning from my boss, "To cut meat, you must pay attention to the machine blade. A small default of attention on your part, just a blink, is enough to get your hand cut. I saw people come here with their two hands and leave with a few fingers missing."

I was cutting and delivering meat from 8 a.m. to 9 p.m., six days a week, and was also keeping the place clean. At first, I was a bit reluctant to do so much. But leaving this job would have been suicidal. I had no problem convincing myself of this, and I was always singing a few songs of mbalax from Senegal during my morning walk to the butcher shop. I was walking in sync with my music, my country, my heart.

Sunday was payday. Need I say it was my favorite day of the week? I was making $150 a week. In two weeks as an apprentice butcher I was making more than a Dakar high school teacher in one month. Even though I was aware of the difference in the cost of living, I couldn't help thinking that I had a good salary.

The first pay Sunday was the most beautiful day in my life. It was the morning. An icy cold wind was blowing in my face, stinging my eyes, but I could see the sun, the shiny sun. I was walking, money in hand, to Western Union. I had noticed their branch as soon as I had arrived, and was dying to get in. I walked up to the teller. A heavy woman stared at me from behind her small glasses. I said loudly, articulating carefully, that I wanted to send money. She handed me a form to fill out. There were not a lot of people so she let me do it in front of her and we proceeded, with solemnity, through the glass window.

"Yes, "I said. "The name of the recipient is Yacine Niang, born Yacine Diop. I am her son, Thione." I spelled her name proudly. In a few hours, my mother would have the equivalent of 100,000 CFA to put away in her little bag.

"Sean?" The woman sighed, slightly fed up with our exotic African names.

"T-H-I-ON-E Niang."

"The town is…?"

"Kaolack!" I said proudly. "It is my birth town. That's where I grew up," I said with enthusiasm.

She lifted her eyes from her screen, looked at me and smiled. I suppose my happiness was communicative because I had not expected this change of attitude from that woman with glasses and her hair in a tight bun.

"The amount is a hundred dollars, right? Your fees will be twenty-two dollars and fifty-six cents. What is your password?"

I looked at her, puzzled.

"Yes," she said seeing my surprise, "the secret word that your mother will use."

"Dieureudieuf" I told her, which means "thank you" in Wolof.

The lady with glasses handed me a receipt and told me to communicate the reference number and the amount to my mother, so that she could get the money.

On my way out, I stopped and looked at the sun. In spite of the cold, its rays were warming me up. I thought about my mom who would also enjoy the rays of the same sun. We were connected by nature, connected by a promise, connected by a prophecy. Mam Thione had predicted it, I had promised it, my mother had dreamed of it. She had never left my thoughts and now I was taking care of her for the first time in my life. I could no longer stand the thought that she was handling the household chores that were so exhausting to her. With my money wires, she would be able to hire a cleaning lady to do the housework, which would let her rest. Also, I sent $20 to my father so that he would pray for me. I did that because it was my mother's wish. To comply with tradition, I did it without any opposition. Respect for my mother, my philosophy and my principles, helped me get the necessary distance to show clemency towards my father. Who would have known that barely a month ago I was penniless and completely lost? Who would have known what the future held for us?

I had hoped for this day for almost my entire life, since I was twelve; from now on my mother would no longer need to slave away to care for a household of over thirty people. Waking up at 5 a.m., then pushing, pulling, dusting, prodding, nursing, cooking, lifting, fetching water, washing: all that until 10 p.m. without a thank you or a mark of appreciation. At last, she would be able to rest, because her son Thione had transferred money! It was not a secret expectation. I had expressed it to my mother numerous times. She would reply with blessings. I called my mother to give her the details of the transfer and to tell her that with God's help, I would keep my commitment.

Every night, in bed, I would calculate what I would do with my earnings. I had the moral satisfaction of being useful.

My projects and my phone conversations with my mother were a reminder of a section of The Poor Man's Son, a novel by Algerian writer Mouloud Feraoun. I had read the book back when I was hanging out at the French cultural center in Dakar. "I can still buy two sheep. We are two. Ce n'est pas au-dessus de nos forces. Au printemps, nous vendrons les bœufs pour acheter une paire plus petite. Nous vendrons aussi trois moutons, nous pourrons avoir une vache. Nous aurons également un peu d'huile en plus de notre consommation. L'été prochain, j'irai avec l'âne vendre des légumes pendant que tu t'occuperas des animaux avec tes sœurs. Bientôt nous remplacerons l'âne par un mulet. Je me livrerai alors au commerce. Tu m'accompagneras de temps en temps dans les marchés pour te mettre au courant. Je crois que grâce à Dieu, nous ne serons plus malheureux." I was very grateful to my parents. Even though I hadn't gotten any help from them in a long time, they were now supporting a good chunk of the expenses related to my son, and were contributing to his education. My mother especially.

Jet lag was still bothering me. I was sleepy during the day, and restless at night. It was mostly at night that my concerns were the most nagging: all my obligations, all my responsibilities, my education, my little salary, utilities to pay, my family's expectations in Kaolack.

I was having a hard time immersing myself in this new world, and adapting to this new way of life. In spite of my curiosity, I was struck with an uneasiness due to all these changes. I had lost my bearings. In Senegal, I was used to eating with the entire family from a large bowl of thiebou dieune. The time of ataya was an opportunity for gathering with friends and parents. Over there, you could spend twenty minutes in greetings only! I could talk and eat peanuts with Tonton Sorano for an hour. I could spend the entire Saturday at my friend Fatima's. Everything that seemed basic, even mundane in Dakar was dearly missed and seemed indispensable.

In New York, people greet each other with a quick "Hi," you eat with your eyes on the clock, sometimes while walking. Back in my country, I would see families, here only individuals. Would I get used to it? At night, my tutor Ass was driving his cab, and I was alone in the apartment. The second Sunday I was paid, I decided to take the subway for the first time and to go to Manhattan. There, I would be able to take photos and send them to my family: irrefutable proofs that would clear up the mind of those who kept wondering about the effectiveness—or not—of my presence in the USA. I bought a disposable camera for $15. The supermarket could have the prints ready in five days. Once at the Gunhill subway station, I had to choose between the various subway lines. I learned very quickly that even New Yorkers get lost quite often. One passenger, who had the same problem, offered to bring me to a police officer. The lady, very nicely, asked me where I wanted to go.

"Manhattan."

"Where in Manhattan?" she said in her American accent, fast and hard to understand.

"Manhattan!"

"But Manhattan is huge!"

"Anywhere in Manhattan."

"Time Square is a good area.

"Ok, then I will go to Time Square."

I went to Time Square, and I saw the America I had dreamed of! Skyscrapers, hotdog stands, yellow cabs, hundreds of pedestrians crowding the wide sidewalks just like in movies, people waiting at the light before crossing the street—in that scene, I instantly thought of Dakar, of our streets without (back then) a single traffic light. I saw that traffic in New York was obeying driving rules, when the main rule in Dakar is that there is no rule. Also, there were no police officers on street corners, looking for a pedestrian or driver to racketeer in peace. That's a common occurrence in Senegal. Like Eddie Murphy's character in the movie "Coming to America." I was flabbergasted, astonished, and was staring at skyscrapers so much that my neck hurt. But people were not talking or laughing. Although it was a Sunday, they all seemed in a hurry. It was a heavy atmosphere for me, who came from a place where people take their time. I befriended a man from Ivory Coast, just like that, on the street. We had noticed each other. Happy with the fact that we could speak the same language, we took photos of one another in front of the buildings. We were complying with a tradition established by several generations of African immigrants. Even when you live in a ghetto in the host country, you take photos in front of the best places in town. Of course, in the most mythical places! These are the photos you send back to your home country, and that your parents will show to their neighbors who, out of bitterness, had secretly hoped that you would fail. I walked a bit further and fortuitously, ended up in front of the United Nations, where flags from all the nations were flying in the wind. I looked for my flag, going over all the other ones before stopping on the American flag.

After a few hours in pursuit of the America of my dreams, I went to Harlem, on 116th Street, famously known as the Senegalese area. I could hear young people speak Wolof. They were talking in small groups and were preparing foaming tea, like in Senegal. Mothers, the very antithesis of American women in jeans, wore African boubous. There were restaurants with African names, (Baobab, Keur Kiné), with a replica of the very famous fast food place Les Ambassades, also in Dakar, where Fatima used to buy my hamburgers. I could hear Youssou N'dour's latest hits. It was really "Little Senegal," hence the movie by Rachid Bouchareb about this community.

Often in Dakar, over tea, everybody says a bit of what they heard about Western countries or the United States. This is how I had heard about this Senegalese neighborhood. Its reputation was welldeserved.

Since my arrival two weeks sooner, I was eating Senegalese food for the first time—a large plate of thiebou dieune, then tea to finish with the famous tasse à palabre. I felt like I had hit the jackpot—I was in the United States without being deprived of Senegal.

I spoke to Fatima and told her about my day, adding that I had seen a replica of Les Ambassades. We were often reminiscing the still fresh memories of our days together. It was a great day of discovery, made even nicer by my conversation with Fatima.

After three weeks spent endangering my hands every day at the butcher's, Ass offered a better job. Ben Niasse, a grandson of the spiritual guide, had been promoted to manager of a Mexican restaurant called Chevy's in New Rochelle. Ben, who had been one of my father's students in Kaolack, recruited me right away. But my accent, deemed incomprehensible, was confining me to the cleaning and dishwashing tasks. Waiting tables was for highschool kids who worked during their time off.

Ben a role model for success. He had all the attributes of success: Impeccable clothing, a nice apartment, a big Land Cruiser. He was the one overseeing the jobs of young immigrants to the US. He was a sort of liaison, like an ambassador between Senegal and the United States. He was helpful, actively contributing to the success of the Senegalese. He was like an uncle, a tutor for all: he was what I wanted to be.

My first days as a cleaning technician were very enriching in the literal sense. In the restaurant, every time I was busing a table, after a customer had left, I would find and pocket coins and five- and ten-dollar bills. I was energetic and speedy, characteristics my boss noticed and encouraged. The Latino guy, who had the same job as I did, was being criticized more and more for his slowness. No one knew that the real motivation for my enthusiasm was the tips I was collecting. At the end of the month, the manager, Ben, gathered all the staff in the kitchen and listened to the waiters' protests. It was an emergency meeting, during which the waiters, exclusively paid on tips, threatened to quit.

"We don't know where our tips go, we're not making anything!" one of them said.

"Wait! The tips I pick up aren't mine?"

"You are taking them?" the staff asked, angry they'd congratulated me for my swiftness without suspecting my monetary motivation.

"These tips are not for you! They explained before warning me: Don't touch any dough. You clean up and that's it. You clean up and you leave, okay?

"No tips! Ever!" said another.

This situation deeply disappointed me because I was already riding my American dream. But I had to submit. In that precious month I had made $800 per week. I had been able to call my family more often, to buy a pair of sneakers and to reward myself with a New York Yankees game at the stadium—I had quite a lifestyle. God bless America! it was like a mantra, like a song that I would repeat over and over while cleaning: every week, with my $150 salary and my $800 in tips, I was making as much as a Senegalese politician!

I understood that in order to reach my American dream, I would have to be a little more patient. I went back to my $150 per week, sometimes enhanced with an extra $20 or $30 from the waiters. I learned many years later, by traveling around the world, that tips are mandatory in the US, but are considered an option in France and are downright insulting in Japan.

Except for this incident, I got accustomed, at last, quite well to my new life. This is what I thought until I had to visit a doctor in the Bronx hospital, because of a painful belly ache. The diagnosis from the doctor was pathetic: "You are eating too much meat M. Niang! You are not the first African to whom this is happening, I have seen other cases like you."

Back home in Kaolack, only the wealthy could eat meat because it was expensive, moreso than fish or any other food in our diet. When Ass Dieng had told me that in New York, meat was more affordable than fish, I had thought the world was going crazy, although in the end, malnutrition was equally affecting us. In Africa we are sometimes malnourished or underfed with terrible deficiencies due to the low nutritional value of our food. In the US, it is also possible to experience malnutrition, but because of too much sugar, fat, and preservatives, a lack of variety—and not enough fruit and vegetable. I was the victim of a sort of malnutrition. By consuming so much meat, I had neglected fruit, vegetables and grains, all ingredients that provide vitamins and fiber and are essential for a balanced diet. I had to resist this little weakness. Obviously meat was not my stomach's friend! This was difficult because in Kaolack, meat consumption was like a kind of social symbol that separates the rich from the poor. When I was young, when my brothers and I were eating meat, we would not wash our hands before returning to school, so that we could tell our friends we had had meat. As proof, we would extend our hand so that the most skeptical could sniff the seasoned smell of our latest meaty experience.

A few days later, it was Cinco de Mayo celebrated on "May 5th by the Mexican community. This celebration commemorates the victory of the Mexican government troops led by General Ignacio Zaragoza over the conservative government troops and the French expeditionary troops in the battle of Puebla on May 5, 1862." That celebration was almost the equivalent of a declaration of independence.

Chevy's was a Mexican place, and we were swamped with customers. The restaurant had been decorated for the occasion and all the staff wore Mexican colors. There was a salsa band playing the most famous hits. I had never set foot in Mexico but the restaurant had been so transformed by all the animation that I felt like I was there. The fondness of American patrons for this day was proof of American diversity, of the easiness with which this people happily and candidly celebrates other cultures. I understood that the visa only lets you enter the country; but the bonds you forge, the friendships you develop, and the beauty of human interactions obliterate the distance separating you from your kind, and in my case were softening the nostalgia of my country.

In my first group of friends, there was Christie, an American, black highschool student who was a waitress in the restaurant. I loved the New York accent of this young woman born in Georgia. Christie was very attracted to African culture, and had told me that her senior year teacher wanted me to come share with the students about the particularities of Senegalese culture. I accepted readily, proud to be an African and honored to share my knowledge and my experience with American people, and curious to learn more about my host country. Our talks were productive and surprising. Questions were popping out of all twenty-four students. Their concerns ranged from climate to family to customs. A young man asked a series of unexpected questions such as, "Is it true that African people live in the jungle? How do you live with wild animals? How do you dress?"

The audience had a hard time believing that in Senegal, like in any other African countries, there are cities, that I had never seen any wild animals, which are often in zoos or reservations, and that we dressed pretty much like I had dressed that morning.

For them, Africa was a giant zoo where Africans enjoyed traditional dancing with monkeys and constantly made a scene.

It was my first speech in the United States. This experience, cheered on by my small audience, inspired and encouraged me to go on and triggered in me a strange feeling: a sensation of harmony and truthfulness stemming from this very specific form of interaction. Before this presentation, I was just a Senegalese immigrant who wanted to make a little money for his family in Kaolack. From then on, I wanted more. I was feeling capable of something bigger, more ambitious. I was feeling in me the drive to approach people, to talk to them. The sleeping activist in me was stirring, the academic year was fast approaching. Meanwhile, I was still washing dishes in New York.

Learn to adapt from different situations, experiences, and people, without comparing yourself to others. Above all, maintain a sense of humor; this will enable you to deal with complex situations. Seek opportunities to encounter 'the other,' whatever it may be, as positive learning experiences where you can develop a range of relationships founded on reciprocity. Since childhood, enthusiasm for learning new things has always guided my steps. Our 'otherness' can be employed as an asset, projecting us beyond the current situation, into a better future.

CHAPTER XII

CLEVELAND, OHIO

"Every human group takes its richness in communication, mutual support and solidarity for the common goal of individual development with respect for differences." Françoise Dolto

Excited to go to college, and careful to remain within the timeframe of my immigrant status, I prepared to leave New York. The opening of the college was planned for August. Ben and Ass Dieng had recommended I take a Greyhound bus to get to Ohio. The imam of the mosque of Medina Baye in Kaolack was visiting in Manhattan, and because I was from Kaolack, I went to meet him. He told me that one of his friends, called Daoud, also an imam, lived in Cleveland. He was a natural and phoned him to say that he expected him to provide me with temporary living arrangements in Cleveland.

So I bid farewell to New York, Ben, Ass, and Christie, gathered the things I had acquired since my arrival, and took a bus to my real destination in the United States, my academic destination. I had around nine hundred dollars in savings and was ready to move forward. In mid-July of 2000, on a great sunny afternoon, I traveled hundreds of kilometers to discover the rich landscape and varied panoramas of the United States. I was going to Ohio, but was impressed with the mountains of Pennsylvania, as well as by the infrastructures. As a matter of fact, highways were large, and roads were well maintained; it was a simple and quiet journey, without any hassle or surprise. I was wondering if my arrival in Cleveland was going to be that simple, if the city was going to be welcoming, if there was a large and tightly knit Senegalese community. There I was once again on the path to uncertainty, to a future full of hope and questions.

The ride was eight hours long, and six had already elapsed when I thought of Christie's words. She had not recommended I go to Cleveland. She thought it was like a little village, an area that was a few years back compared to New York. Two hours later, I understood what she meant. Cleveland was an old town, empty and under-urbanized. I was shocked to see a dead city with no one around. In Africa, people wait for urbanization, not the other way round. Imam Daoud had sent one of his followers to get me at the bus terminal. He was an American black man like you see on TV, a fifty-year-old with a beautiful Cadillac. We went to his place, where we had dinner with his wife, daughter, and son. The meal was friendly and the welcome was warm; but our conversation was limited because I had a hard time understanding them. My English was not up to speed. The following day, they drove me to the Cuyahoga Community College in Cleveland. Once there, I met Pamela, at the department of international affairs of the University. She was pretty and had a je ne sais quoi that was reassuring and inspired trust. Pamela was made for that job. She had been my contact in my exchanges with the university and was always dedicated. She explained that the school had no dorms and that I should contact the YMCA, a Christian association that could help. She helped me secure a small studio with a monthly rent of $420.

There is a tight relationship between the words poverty and smallness. I had left a small house in Kaolack for a small room at my grandmother's in Dakar, then my brother's small apartment, and there again, a small studio. I had always heard people with limited resources express their ambitions in those words: "to have a little wife, a little house, a little car." Me, I've always wanted a great destiny, and this small studio was a mandatory phase. There was a small bed, a fridge and a desk, in all much more comfort than I could have dreamed of in Dakar.

The following day, Pamela called me to her office. She told me that, having obtained the visa in January, and showed up at the university only six months later, I was at risk of losing the visa. Which, to make a long story short, meant that the odds of going back to Senegal were very high. I was filled with anxiety, feeling run down. She explained the possibilities that were mine: either going out of the country to Canada, Great Britain or Senegal, and then coming back, or writing a letter to the immigration services to explain the reasons for my delay. Pamela did not recommend the second option, because, she said, "In ninety-nine percent of cases, immigrants that make this kind of request only get a refusal, along with a deportation to their country."

The option that she, the expert, was finding too risky for me was the only one I could consider, because I had only $900, of which $420 would pay the rent, and no extra money to spend on a trip. Pamela thought my choice was daring, if not crazy, for someone who really wanted to study in the US. Indeed, this decision was not conventional, but it was the only possible venue for me. I was betting all my arguments, my honesty and my power of persuasion on this one percent of a chance, in a form that I had filled out with the utmost concentration.—a one percent chance of obtaining a favorable answer from the immigration services. Only three months after my arrival, I had to wait two weeks to know if I should pack my suitcase or if I was at last going to pursue my life project.

Those were two very difficult weeks, with my mind tortured by many fears. What would I do back in my country? What to do if I was deported by my host country? I thought I was already settled, but I might have to pick up and leave. I might deceive the family expectations. What would I say to my mother? What would I say to the neighbors? What would I do once in Senegal? How could I go home when I had barely sown the seeds of hope? Seeds that had not even had time to germinate? This unlivable situation, was above all shameful, like for the majority of African immigrants. As a matter of fact it is better considered to not leave one's country at all than to be deported back to it. It is a situation that shames the entire family, sometimes leading to exile. Indeed, some opt to live as prisoners, stuck abroad clandestinely rather than return home free. But this wouldn't be my fate. I was refusing to consider it. I confided in my mother and in Fallou. And they both did the only thing they could do for me: pray.

Two weeks later, Pamela announced that the committee had decided in my favor. I was going to stay and study. I was relieved.

Unable to pay the $3,000 of tuition costs in one go, or even $1,500 per semester, I obtained from the school administration the possibility of paying for my classes on a monthly basis, for $375 per month. For that first year, I absolutely had to take English classes.

On back to school day, I had no balance whatsoever allowing me to be serene. In the auditorium, I was thinking of the way I would manage to come to class, eat, and buy warm clothing for colder weather, because of what the old man had said at the American embassy: "It gets cold over there in Ohio." I had to find a job at all costs. Once out of class, I would pour over the help wanted ads in search of employment. It was becoming an urgent need.

I walked from 22nd Street (Downtown), where I lived, to First Street (Time Square) to look for a job. In my quest, I had the good idea to stop at the Marriott Hotel in Cleveland. They gave me and the other applicants forms to fill out, and the hotel restaurant recruited me as a busboy. My experience at Chevy's had helped.

I started work the following morning. Just in time, because I had no money left at all. Fallou had sent me $200 spent on school-related expenses.

On the first day they gave me a shirt and a tie to start my service and took my measurement to order me a uniform. I have always loved "dressing up," i.e. wearing a suit, and if this job provided the opportunity to do so, it was all for the best. I was going to the Marriott every day at 6 a.m. The hotel was always fully booked, thanks to the fame of the Cleveland Clinic, renowned for its cardiovascular care. In the afternoon I would go to class. And lastly, at night, I was combating sleep to study for classes and to think.

Approximately two months after my start at the hotel, a highranking Algerian political figure came to the Clinic for his health, but stayed at the hotel. He was accompanied by a large delegation. James, the restaurant's young manager, assembled us in a meeting to discuss an urgent situation that made our waiters unhappy. The Algerians took too long to order their food, because they couldn't speak English, and furthermore they would never leave any tip. Another tipping problem, except this time, it was not my fault!

James asked if anyone could speak French. I raised my hand humbly and was surprised to see that I was the only one speaking the language of Molière. I was immediately promoted, as a maître d' specifically assigned to the Algerian delegation. I filled that role successfully. The Algerian guests gained a better appreciation for the quality of the hotel services, and became generous in their tipping, which made me more likable in the eyes of my coworkers. As a reward, I was promoted to host manager of the restaurant, in charge of coordinating work for all the waiters. This time I had a better suit, and this motivated me. I liked suits. Just like Mam Thione, I loved a good custom-made suit.

I was making $7 an hour, which was already better than the $5 as a cleaning person.

One day, James called me and said I was too intelligent to work at the door of a restaurant.

"Why don't you teach French? There is a real need for that," he said, encouraging me with a nod.

"This is nice, James, thank you… But I have no teaching diploma, and anyway I don't know anyone to help me with this type of project," I said, realistically.

He told me about the Plain Dealer, a Cleveland publication where I could find ads for available positions.

After a few days of research, I found an ad from a school with an "immediately available" position. I went there right away and met with the principal. During the conversation, I found out that the school belonged to Imam Daoud, who had helped me upon my arrival in Ohio. It was a strange coincidence. Was this a wink from destiny? The conversation was interesting but became downright fascinating when he mentioned that my salary would be $30,000 per year. Converting this amount in FCFA yielded approximately, at the time, 21,000,000 FCFA. In less than five minutes, I already had projects: I was going to buy houses in Kaolack, and also cars to get there of course! I called my mother to tell her that I was a millionaire.

"Millionaire? How did this happen?"

I found a job as a French teacher, and I'll be paid around twenty-one million per year."

"Congratulations, my Thione!"

"Get information about the cost of land in Kaolack, I want to buy a lot of land. Acres and acres—we will plant as far as the eye can see. Mother, also get an estimate for renovating my grandfather's house. Don't spare any expense. It is very important, and I have the money to pay."

Two weeks later, it was time to get our salary. The administration manager gave us envelopes with our check inside. I discreetly left the room to open my envelope. Very excited at the prospect of becoming a millionaire, I tore the envelope, took a deep breath with my eyes closed, exhaled, opened my eyes and saw my check of $700! I had gotten only $700. There had to be a mistake, so I checked the contents of the envelope one more time, there might be some other check—but, no. Attached to my meager check was a statement spelling out the various deductions made to various taxes. Furious, I stormed into the administration office to express my anger.

"Miss, I am not happy with my check! Why do you pay me only seven hundred dollars? If you must deduct money from my salary, the least you should do is ask me. You should first find out if I feel like paying these taxes! And it so happens that I don't feel like paying them."

She had me sit down, and explained with a smirk what each deduction was about.

"This is how it is here. You don't choose to pay your taxes or not. You pay and that's that. Welcome to America!"

I took the time to open a bank account to cash the check, and told my mother to forget about my financial ambitions.

"Mother, we must wait before buying land as far as the eye can see. For Grandfather's house, put away the estimate. With what I am making now, I can send you money every month and pay for my university, but that's about it. I am not a millionaire yet. Here, they give you a lot of money, but they take it all back."

Additionally, the deadline for repaying my debt for the plane ticket from Dakar to New York was already reached, and I had to pay it back. My mother and I had a good laugh at our naiveté.

In light of these situations, it seemed appropriate to ask for guidance when the context was unclear, or when facing adversity. Misinterpretations and misunderstanding can lead to unfortunate consequences and compromise the future.

CHAPTER XIII

BACK TO THE SOURCE

"The real novelty is always born in the homecoming." Edgar Morin

I was just trying to understand the American way of life, but one encounter helped me better understand how this atypical country worked.

I met Joy unexpectedly on the day of the Thanksgiving holiday. This happened at the bus Greyhound bus station, where I had gone to greet a friend. The bus was late, and I saw stopped a beautiful young African-American girl of Indian origin. She seemed lost. Anxious to assist in the filling, I approached and introduced myself. She wanted to go to Columbia and had to change buses, but was inadvertently missed his correspondence. Without money, she knew no one and appeared lost and hesitant about what she could do. Just in case, I offered my help and left her my phone number, stating clearly that she could call me in case of difficulties. She took my number, but declined any other form of assistance, including my proposal to host it for the night which promised. Much later that night, Joy ended up calling me. She did not find any place to sleep and has agreed to share our apartment; I was really happy to help. It is a little later, during a weekend that Joy invited me to go to his family in the countryside, 45 miles from Cleveland. I was then an old and modest car, a Dodge Intrepid, which I had bought for a small fee associated with my limited means. Joy's family greeted me pleasantly. His parents were humble people. In his family, it was not customary to consider a university education: neither she nor her siblings had not had the opportunity. It just was not envisaged at any time, for lack of examples in their surroundings and information about the possibilities of access to higher education.

I saw Joy for a year. We were inseparable, she could finish my sentences and I could finish her thoughts. Although she had a cautious nature, she loved me with endless love. However her caution had another side that helped me greatly: it opened my eyes. This precious realization, stemmed by Joy, was what "finished me off" about her. I would pick her up at her home and we would go to school together. It was relatively simple until winter came and snow appeared.

The first snow I saw made me happy. I had only seen it on TV, so many times. One day I woke up, and saw through the curtains what seemed like snow, so I rushed to the window to make sure. Yes, it was snow! Light, soundless, discreet, it was delicately covering the ground, the roofs, the trees, and the heads of the occasional pedestrian in the street. Excited, I hastily got my clothes and shoes on, and went out to feel and touch this gift of nature. I was barely outside before I'd slipped on the stoop. I was barely upright that I slipped again—my poor choice of shoes was punishing me, and I was advised to buy shoes with studs. Another expense, I thought. But this time it would be a special expense because snow was my friend. Mysterious, with a pure color, with each snowflake different from the previous one, snow was both solid and liquid, and ended up evaporating. What was the lifespan of a snowflake? It was fascinating and magical. Snow was definitely my friend. I too was a snowflake. Many hurdles, I knew, were on my path to the future, but just like a snowflake, I had to adapt to my environment. This is how, in the falling snow, I took my first step and after lots of thinking, decided to ask Joy to marry me. A lonely and isolated snowflake is only a lost snowflake and represents nothing. But two snowflakes together indicate a change of season. Joy would be the snowflake with which I would herald a change, a change for the better.

So we got married in winter, on Christmas Day. We had known each other for one year. She moved in with me and transformed my apartment into a home. She was supportive and was finding in me a pillar of stability. To her I represented a determination, a motivation, a discipline that she had liked as soon as we had met. She shared with me her knowledge of America, her culture, her history, and in return I did the same about Senegal, but adding a specific touch: telling about my values and principles, to which she adhered. We were in perfect harmony from the beginning, a close-knit couple that had learned to discover, respect and love each other during our entire marriage.

The school where I was teaching served mostly young black students, children of poor parents growing up in very complex family backgrounds.

Most of them were raised by a single parent: a young mother struggling with several small jobs, day and night. These young people had no concept of respect for the adults. They would fight and insult each other. Daily, I would witness their shocking violence. I couldn't help compare the overcrowded Senegalese classrooms, filled with one hundred more or less rambunctious students, with the classes of twenty-five uncontrollable students here. Sometimes students were arrested for violent behavior or drug dealing. Sometimes students would bring guns into class, which would, of course, create real panic. Several tragedies involving guns take place every year in schools. In December 2012, a shooting in a school in Newtown, Connecticut, killed twenty-seven people, of which twenty were small children. President Obama said that this day had been the saddest of his presidency.

In Senegal, there are thousands of students in every school, but no one is searched. On the other hand in Cleveland, the school's eight hundred students were searched individually every day.

Here, young people always have something to say when in Africa, the teacher is simply always right. Here, I saw teachers who had problems with their administration simply for having raised their voice when speaking to a child. This would be unthinkable in Africa, where a child doesn't belong to his parents, but to the community that raises him, without a specific mandate from the parents. It is a social convention. In my opinion, American parents had a lax concept of strictness. Since I was only twenty-two, my sixteen- to eighteen-year-old students were feeling close to me, and thought of me more as one of their kind than as an educator. But make no mistake. I was the teacher and had no qualms exercising my responsibilities with consistency and firmness when necessary. Therefore, I would summon the parents of the least disciplined kids in my classroom, in order to talk to them. I took real pleasure in being a mediator between parents and children, aware that I myself was the product of the pains that can stem from a conflict between parents. In their eyes, I was a different teacher, young, nice, firm, but also funny and exotic because of my accent. I was entertaining the students, who had about Africa the same questions than the highschoolers in Christie's school.

Through our discussions, I learned slang, the street English, which made me discover another America, another language that got me closer to this new community. The interaction was more sincere, more authentic that way, because they spoke with me heartily and honestly, assertively and confidently, as if I were from the community.

Daoud Shabazz, the head of the school, was like a book of American history from 19xx to 19xx. American, black and proud of it, he loved talking about his past as an activist within the Black Panthers, or along Malcolm X. And with the same enthusiasm, he loved to recount his patriotic involvement through his military career. Lastly, he had fought for the civil rights of blacks and minorities. His nickname was Diablo. He was rigorous and with great human value, always available for young people. He had started a class for reinserting young people right out of jail. "Youth in our community often get on the path to jail if they're lucky, or to the graveyard if they're not lucky. We must reverse this trend by turning these young people into role models for those at risk of making the same mistakes."

The program was successful, because it enabled those freshly released to avoid returning to their natural habitat, the ghetto. It was protecting them from their environment.

I was shocked, moved and saddened to see so many youths going to jail. It seemed that incarceration had become a rite of passage that they had to go through to be respected, taken seriously, to become men! In Senegal, going to jail was the worst sentence, not at all an option. Going to jail was synonymous with sanction, failure, separation, shame!

At the end of the school year, I suggested to Daoud that we select the best fifteen students in the French class to bring them to Africa, where they would encounter another reality. It would also be an opportunity to learn more about their ancestry, their roots. I wanted to expose them to something different. So, for my students, I proposed Senegal.

The trip took place during the month of May, and we brought twenty-two computers, no longer needed by our school, as a gift to the Lycée Blaise Diagne, which I had left one year earlier.

I was surprised to see that none of my students had a passport. But, unlike for me, theirs was issued within twenty-four hours of their application. I was very excited to go back to my country as a teacher, and as a sponsor bringing computers for young Senegalese students. Now, I didn't think myself a hero, far from it, but rather like a son of Kaolack coming to share some of his good fortune with his peers. Never, in my craziest dreams, could I have imagined all this happening so quickly. After only one year! I was in a pretty fast lane: I knew it and was proud of it. I was also honored to see my family again in such circumstances. I couldn't sleep, so happy was I to see my mother again, my son, Anta, Fatima, Amadou and—my country.

We boarded quietly, the trip was uneventful and we arrived at Dakar Airport where my students were welcomed by their Senegalese pen pals. I had organized a program of exchange letters between the students so that the Americans could better get used to our pace and culture, and so that they find allies and friends to explain things. Because, after all, I couldn't lend a listening ear to every student at all times.

At first, the acclimation was tough, but over time my group got used to its new environment: the spicier food, the music with unknown instruments, and the endless conversations around a cup of tea!

I still remember the trick I played on my mother by arriving in Senegal. I had not warned her of my visit, and thought it would be a good surprise, although Joy had recommended otherwise. One phone call only and my mother was imagining the worse. "Thione! Oh my God! Have you been deported? What have you done my son, what have you done?" Poor her, she imagined that I had been deported and that I was back forever. I reassured her and promised to see her the following day, because I had to get my students settled first. I was dying to see my family again!

After three hours on the bus, I was back in Kaolack! Colors were different, more vivid, although covered with a film of red dust. Trees were in bloom, and smells of food were already floating in the air. I so wanted Joy to be there, but she couldn't come. She already knew my mother, with whom she already shared a bond, my father, my past, but I would have liked her to see where I was from, I would have liked to show her my house, the house of Mam Thione, the soccer field or the neighborhood of Medina Baye. Next time, I thought—next time. The bus stopped at the terminal, and I got off. Once outside, a whole group of my family was there, horsing around, whistling, and clapping: I didn't know where to hide. It was a simple joke because it was only me, but I must say I was moved. Even those who had criticized me and had not encouraged me were there. I walked to the bus luggage compartment, and got my six suitcases! Yes, I had managed to bring a little bit of America back here in Kaolack. I wanted to share the fruit of my humble success with all my loved ones. Gifts were immediately handed out, and at last I went home. Not Mam Thione's house—my house, which

I had left six years earlier to never return because my father had banished me.

Moved, I discovered the new decor. I could see my mom's little touches here and there—a curtain here, pillows there. The help brought me to the living room and I waited for my mother to join me. But instead, I saw my father. He came in, saluted me silently and sat down at my right without uttering a word. But his silence was eloquent. It said, Welcome, I was wrong about you and I am sorry. His gaze never met mine but I knew. I could feel that a wind of peace had blown over the Niang household. I looked at his hands. He had aged. His posture was less erect, he was no longer the same man. We both had changed. And while I was trying to find something to say, my mother appeared. Beautiful, with a rested face, dressed in a white outfit, with a smile, she opened her arms and tenderly hugged me, saying in a low voice: "Welcome home, Thione. Welcome home." I offered her my gifts and those sent by Joy. We had a family lunch. We talked of everything I had missed during my absence, of everything we hoped the future would bring with the help of God—and before I left, over a wonderful ataya, my mother blessed me. I returned to Dakar. This time I had a destination, I was not going on an adventure, begging God to help me, hoping someone would house and feed me. This time I was on my way to Dakar, where I was needed, where my young flock was waiting for me.

The stay lasted almost one month, during which my students were able to see youths who also lived in difficult conditions but didn't necessarily fall into self-destruction. Also, a visit to the island of Gorée and to the village of Kouta Kinté in Gambia prompted a huge emotional response in them.

This trip was a magical time for me, and although it was not enough to turn around the lives of these youths, it probably helped. Back in Cleveland, they were more serene, calmer, and less combative. I kept in touch with them, and I am happy to report that today most have managed to resist the call of the ghetto. They are good fathers with good jobs, whose experience in Africa helped put things in perspective, free themselves from the social and emotional burden, and get rid of their weighty past to welcome a future only they could create.

After two years working at the school of Daoud Shabazz, I left for another school called the Imani Institute. To avoid issues of availability, I had the status of an external consultant. I had created a business providing bilingual education in French and Spanish. I had found someone to teach Spanish, and I kept teaching French. Called Thione Niang International, this small company helped me build self-confidence. I was on a trend, aware of the long way I had come, aware of the long path to go, grateful to this formidable country for everything it had given me and for the way my life had been changed. I had one desire, driven in part by my gratefulness, to give a bit of my time to my community and help those in my immediate surroundings do a little better.

I had one lawyer friend, Reggie Maxton. He was sporting his fifty years with great elegance and was treating me as an equal, although he was twice my age. Organizing donations of computers, rice bags or other kind of help would not be enough in the long term. Maxton said, "Get involved in politics. Not to become a politician but to come up with real solutions, leading to real decisions, decisions that will affect the political world and that will touch hundreds and thousands of people. This is how you can really have an impact on people's lives."

But he also pointed out that in American politics, if you make a mistake you are tagged for life, and you don't get a second chance.

"Go with confidence, go with self-esteem, go if you believe in it," he added.

I discussed my new aspirations with Joy. She tried to dissuade me because she thought such a commitment would be fruitless, since politicians were famously ungrateful. "They will use you, but won't help you. And they might try to destroy you when you are no longer useful."

These reservations created a doubt in me for a while, but the need to be an activist became stronger than ever. I researched the two parties in the American political life. I went to the Republican Party headquarters. They gave me general information on their party and an information pamphlet about an upcoming event. I attended, and I asked questions about the foundations and principles of the party. They said they believed anybody had the power to succeed in America, and those who failed were lazy. I was not convinced. I took the same approach to the Democratic Party. There, unlike with the Republicans, I was able to agree with the ideas of the leaders.

In order to better understand the articulations of the American political system, I would often attend the town council meetings in Cleveland. I went there every Monday night for about a year. I knew no one, but these meetings were opened to the public, so I was often there. These meetings strengthened my desire to get into politics.

One day I decided to move to the next phase. Within the town council, the elected official whose ideas I liked best was Zac Reed, a very eloquent young Democrat. At the end of one of the meetings, I went up to him to offer my help for the next campaigns. He quickly dismissed me, saying, "I don't need you."

This first rejection hit me. I started to think that Joy was right in discouraging me from the political crowd. The following Monday I stayed home, trying to devise a strategy. Reggie recommended I talk to Kevin Conwell, another town council member whom he knew well. The meeting took place in better conditions, because Kevin was in love with Africa and therefore had a great openness about him. We exchanged business cards, and he promised to call me. As a matter of fact, his assistant called two weeks later, asking me if I were available to help Kevin Conwell in his campaign. Elections were six months away.

I had no mentor and didn't know much about the social and cultural norms in the United States. I remember that on my first job interview with James at the Marriott, I had kept my eyes down while he would talk to me. This irritated him, and he ended up asking, "Why aren't you looking at me?" In Africa, when an elder speaks, one must not stare at him. It is perceived as a lack of respect. He helped me understand that in America, not looking the other party in the eye indicates a lack of self-confidence. And self-confidence was essential for a politician. You need self-esteem to create political desire and to generate the trust of the people, so that they believe in the change promised by the candidates, Trust! I had to have confidence in myself! Self-esteem!

At that time, I understood the degree to which my biculturalism was an asset. Instead of belittling or dismissing my experience, I leaned on my personal achievements and derived from them inspiration in my future in the United States. I realized that politics motivated me as a mode of action and expression; it was necessary to impact others.

CHAPTER XIV

THANKSGIVING

« The path through the forest is long, but only if you don't like the person you are visiting ». African proverb

I was already caught in the trap of political bulimia. I wanted more canvassing, more contacts with people, more campaigns, and more adrenaline. This was activism, thus volunteering. But in terms of networking and experience, campaigning was well-rewarded. Joy did not share my passion for politics, which she called dangerous. Because of my political commitment, which by the way was not paid in beginning, we had had to leave our cosy little nest to move to a cheaper neighborhood to make ends meet. I could no longer offer Joy something stable, something solid. I was too far in to backtrack now. I was so close to the goal, the goal of becoming a political figure in our community. It was as if we lived on the edge of an ever-threatening volcano. Having lived near volcanos in the past, I knew that the smoke they emit does not necessarily indicate danger, but change. Joy could only see the smoke, only smell the sulfur, and naturally was afraid. She had to trust me. I had survived so many eruptions that, should another happen, I would know how to protect her. The volcanoes that were my father, and Dakar, and the visa, and the university… My entire life had been built near a cliff. I had always lived in the vicinity of the end, of destruction, of despair, but overtime I had managed – especially with Joy's help – to get a bit further from the center of the volcano. I knew what I was doing. I had my faith, my only and ever-present, ever-resourceful ally. And now, there were Joy and a new tiny snowflake called El Hadji Fallou our son, who was just born. I had given him the same first name as my brother FALLOU who lived in Italy, to pay tribute to my big brother. His birth made us both very happy, and strengthened my commitment to politics. "Joy, the reason I am getting into politics is for Fallou to have a future free of the hurdles that plague our youth now".

The experience acquired with Kevin Conwell enabled me to work more effectively for the Cleveland mayoral campaign for Franck Jackson in November 2005. These were nine long and exhausting months during which one had to forgo sleep and family time. Nothing was certain, nothing was a given. I had doubts, of course, I was afraid to make a mistake, to under-perform. But my determination, my passion and my faith, always a source of strength, were supporting me day and night. From March to November, the campaign team of the Mayor, to which I belonged, was extremely united. The vital need to reach our goal was running in our veins. I was the organizer in charge of the young people. My experience as an educator helped me a lot, and the slang I had learned in schools facilitated my contacts with the most fearsome youth gangs.

Within the voters, the atmosphere was not always peaceful. Cleveland was facing a sort of exodus, leaving the city deprived of its businesses, and some jobs had been shipped offshore, for example to China or India. A good portion of the Cleveland population had left to go to other cities offering more jobs. The anger of some was palpable.

I had suggested to the mayor that we stop the bleeding by creating an office specifically targeted at immigrants. That office would offer populations from other states some guidance about our city, which was essential to consider living, working or even creating jobs there.

Young students who were educated in the state universities would leave after graduation. The Mayor approved my proposal and asked me to work on it seriously.

After the announcement of his reelection in November, Mayor Franck Jackson recruited almost all the young volunteers who had supported him, to bring to life the campaign promises that had won him the votes. I was not among them. This seemed unfair, surprising, disappointing. The team spirit that had always prevailed within the group was soon replaced by a sickening form of individualism, with the ultimate goal of getting as close as possible to the Mayor.

Joy had warned me: "Politicians are are not trustworthy." This forecast became painfully real. One of my campaigning companions, got a $69,000 position! This injustice, this favoritism disappointed me enormously. However, the lessons I learned were worth it all; the Mayor clearly said to me: "Money and numbers (votes), these are your friends. If you have neither one nor the other, you are a nobody." The following day, I joined the Young Democrats. That door, slammed in my face, had forced me to change my vision of the world, to broaden my perspective. I decided that if there was not yet a path for me, I would create one.

Since my arrival in the USA I had managed, every month, to send money to my parents for various expenses. My father was already retired and his meager pension as a school principal was not even covering his health expenses. I had stopped my language-education business in order to work exclusively on the Mayor's campaign. Therefore, I had spent one year working as a volunteer, having to live off my savings, which also went to the campaign. My candor ended up costing me a lot. I had the feeling of having taken all the wrong turns, all the bad decisions. However, I couldn't give up that easily. So I kept attending the Town Council Meetings, in the hope that one day, Mayor Franck Jackson would surprise me by offering me a mission. Every day, every precious dollar that I would spend was furthering me from the little kingdom I had created over the past two years. El Hadji was barely six weeks old and I could not even fill the fridge. I couldn't look my wife in the eye. With every passing day, I was losing my honor as a man, my pride as a husband, my responsibility as a father.

Every time my phone rang, I would pray the gods that the call not come from Kaolack. And when the screen showed « Mother », I would not dare to pick up. How could I explain that I couldn't send anything? Nothing! Not even money for rice. How could I explain to my mother, of whom I was the main provider, that she would have to let the cleaning lady go, and herself return to washing pots, doing laundry, and cooking daily for a household of over 20 people ?

I took the cowardly way. I didn't pick up. Every day, I would cry and pray, then go to the Town hall. This lasted six months.

The insecurity of electricity and fuel had often been mentioned as burdensome by the populations who had no money. I was meditating a lot on these thoughts when my gas and electricity were turned off. My car was gathering dust, since I couldn't afford any gas for the tank.

In Cleveland, winters are harsh. Living without heat in this area where the temperature can drop to -26 degrees Celsius in November was simply deadly. Three sweaters and two coats were not enough: I could no longer feel anything: my ears, my hands nor my feet

Some days, I had nothing to eat. At night, I was hoping – but in vain – that a miracle would happen, then I would remember that the early bird gets the worm. So I would go again and again to the town hall.

But I was not in despair, because Thanksgiving was fast approaching. It would be the perfect opportunity to put the sad and the negative aside, be it for one day, in order to reconnect with those I loved. Thanksgiving is a celebration that embodies human warmth, friendship and joy. It is the moment when American families pull out the good old recipes to make pies, roast turkeys and prepare delicious warm drinks including one I especially love: apple cider with a touch of caramel! I was breathing at last, relieved to put all my problems aside, for one night only, and spend the time as pleasantly as possible with my wife and baby. If I worked so hard, it was for them. They were my inspiration, my real shelter. I was going to my peaceful place, my little family nest that in the end I missed so much. Joy was staying with her mother with El Haji for a month only 45mn away from Cleveland. For that special occasion I had bought a small sweet potato pie: the seasonal dessert that Joy loved and hoping to surprise her!

A week from ThanksGiving I had gotten home two hours earlier than scheduled, sitting on the bed, I noticed the open closet: her side of it was empty. "The bassinet! The bassinet is gone!"

It took me some time, but I realized after searching our small apartment a second, then a third time, that Joy came in and took her stuff. She had left with our two-month old son. I was not able to think, it was such a shock.

It was over. She had told me, repeatedly, of her disagreement regarding my political involvement, which she considered selfish and useless. However, she had never given me an ultimatum, never said she would leave me. I admitted having favored my political aspirations; however it was only in the hope of making them proud, of offering them an even better future. And not because I was selfish, naïve or blinded by my ambition: it was because I knew I could make it. I knew I was worthy of my expectations.

So, alone under my covers on this last Thursday of November, on Thanksgiving night, trying to survive the cold, I closed my eyes. I could hear the singing and laughter from my neighbors'. I could smell the spices from their roasted turkey, I could even imagine the taste of nutmeg from their pumpkin pie. My imagination heightened my hunger, and my solitude heightened my bitterness. Rubbing my hands against each other as fast as possible, I tried not to die from the cold. I thought about a proverb from Quebec, which goes "a man without a woman won't survive the winter."

« I am going back to Senegal. Back. » I said out loud. Almost hypnotized by this vapor (from my breath against the cold air), I reviewed this idea: I could, with my diploma, get a job in the administration, create an English-language training center, or teach

English in a high school. But as soon as the vapor disappeared, I gave up this idea, thinking about the son I would have to leave. I thought about my path since Kaolack, and remembered my first departure to the unknown, and the sentence spray-painted on the side of the bus to Dakar.

"When the going gets tough, the tough gets going." John Fitzgerald Kennedy.

The next days, I tried to survive in spite of the lack of everything. My situation lasted six months, after which I decided to break the silence and be brave by confiding into someone. Council member Kevin Conwell was receptive to my despair, and decided to intercede for me and talk to the Mayor. We came across the latter in the town hall stairway. Kevin spoke to the Mayor:

—We must help Thione find a job, he is having a hard time.

— I don't have a job for him, but you, Kevin, you could help, why don't you do it?

I could not understand the detachment of this politician for whom I had sacrificed, or rather lost, everything. I had sacrificed my sleep, spent my days and my savings to try to foster his ideas to the local population. I had been the first to obtain 3300 signatures in three days to help him become a candidate. The entire town had witnessed my loyalty and my assiduity for him. He no longer had the same face.

In the afternoon, Kevin Conwell called me at his home to announce a great piece of news that was going to end my the dark nights. He had, like any council member, the possibility of naming a "Community organizer," whose work was to listen to populations, to report their problems and to follow up on their resolution. I was going to make $30,000 per year thanks to Conwell's allotted budget.

This title was perfect for me. I liked the constant contact with people, and everything you can learn from it. We would organize charitable events to benefit the poorest, who would get donations from city authorities. These gestures were much appreciated and I was, in the eye of the people, the « good guy » who was always there when someone needed him.

I gave a report to the town council every Thursday. This experience helped me regain my self-esteem, because I could read in other people's eyes how much they trusted me. It was thanks to their appreciation that I was able to stand on my two feet again. And then I realized that Joy would never come back to me.

While there are multiple aspects of my life that shape my thoughts and decisions, some of the most important are my two sons and their mothers. I have always tried to give them as much love and support as possible, and thus offset any difficult times they have known because of my choices and mistakes. As for Joy, it means so much to me that she and I were able to quickly restore peaceful and harmonious relations with each other after our parting. And I'm so very proud of her; although it was a huge challenge, she finished her nursing studies and is now working to earn a master's degree, as well.

Joy has ensured my closeness with El Hadji as I carry out my work around the world. She gives him lots of love and a good education; I am grateful for everything she has done, and continues to do. Joy strives to be the best example possible to both El Hadji and his younger brother, who I have adopted— her success is proof that one should never give up.

I am honored by the opportunity my family gives me to live a responsible, rich life of optimism and cooperation; and with these things, I have the support and inspiration to serve others through my work.

Navigating a system that overwhelms and demoralizes you, and still demonstrating the capacity to envision a solution, is a powerful source of serenity and inspiration. I never surrendered to defeat, despite the temptation. I strove to stay grounded, conscious that I could not achieve anything if I did not ardently pursue a solution. After hitting rock bottom of the swimming pool, so to speak, I catapulted myself back to the surface to breathe again.

CHAPTER XV

DOUBLE CULTURE

"Who wants to go unnoticed should not sneeze." African proverb

One very cold and snowy morning in Ohio. In the Carl Stokes federal building in Cleveland, I was about to attend the ceremony for my naturalization.

Several months earlier, the immigration services had called me for my last interview, during which I would take a written and oral test. I had stayed up studying many times, my only respites being frequent conversations with others who had gone through the procedure before. One of my friends, Papis Niang, had become my "coach." He tried to reassure me and prepare me as well as possible. But I was nervous. The first part was the written test—I passed this part fairly easily. The oral part lasted only a few minutes during which they had asked me three questions: The name of capital of the United States, the name of the Attorney General, and the number of Senators in Congress.

Following the instructions I had received, I arrived at 11:00am sharp. I was not expecting to be the only one, but did not expect to see over 400 others in the room, ready to live the same experience. We were there to become American.

I was expecting the process to be more of a chore than an enjoyable experience. Curious to know more, I had spent the previous night searching on the internet for what exactly the ceremony would entail, but no website could have prepared me for what I was going to experience.

As the day went by, I realized that I was going to partake in something both beautiful and special. I was filled with strong love and gratitude for America. At last, I would be part of the American people with whom I had gotten involved by contributing my time and my energy. I had supported my family in Kaolack, my American students, my high school in Dakar, my growing family, my community in Cleveland and the Democratic Party. I had been able, with honor, gratitude and respect, to keep in touch with my two homelands: Senegal and the United States. On that particular day, I was proud to call the USA my country.

As the ceremony commenced, I paid great attention to the instructions delivered by the clerk in charge. Once inside, she waited for everyone to find a place before explaining how the process would unfold: She would call our names, and one by one, in great discipline, we would line up to see her individually. The atmosphere was formal and solemn. After she finished calling all the names, I had a moment of panic: my name was not on the list, because she had not called me. She asked: "Is there anyone here who has not been called?" Immediately I stood and walked up to her.

Her index finger was running over the sheets of paper. She went through three pages before stopping at the top of the fourth;

tapping her finger vigorously on my name, she said "Thione Niang. I found you. There you are". My name was clearly spelled out on the much-vaunted list, and reassured, I returned to my seat. She checked off her list and asked me to surrender my green card, and threw it carelessly into a cardboard box, along with several hundred others.

Awestruck, I looked at all those cards that were no longer important. These cards, in our eyes, are more valuable than diamonds: they enable us, as non-American citizens, to settle and work legally in the United States, without requiring a visa. I realized I would no longer carry the card with me, but in me: I no longer needed it.

Each of us received a packet of information. A strong symbol, we all got an American flag, the "Citizen Almanac," the lyrics of the national anthem, and a copy of the Declaration of Independence of the United States. We were also given civic information about our rights and duties as Americans citizens, and practical information, such as how to apply for a new passport.

The judge who was to preside over the oath of allegiance then arrived, and the ceremony officially started.

I remember the earnest smile of the Pakistani woman who was sitting next to me. In front of us, a woman with a Jamaican accent had turned around with a big smile and a wink. The moment had been dreamed about for so long that we all felt bound together. Bound by our happiness, by the feeling of belonging to the same Nation, we were now fellow citizens.

The judge gave a moving and inspiring speech. "To preside over this ceremony, he said, was [his] way of delivering on America's promise to welcome people, wherever they come from, to keep building a society made better by its multiculturalism". He urged us to work together to the strengthening and betterment of our country. To illustrate his point, he read the names of all the countries whose immigrants would be naturalized, and each person would stand up when the name of their original country was called. I was the only one from Senegal that day. Our diversity was our strength.

To wrap up the legal process, the judge invited us to perform our first act as American citizens: it was to pledge our allegiance to the American flag. We were about 400 people, reciting the oath in unison. I will never forget the size of the brightly colored flag: it was huge! Huge!! My eyes filled with tears. We were all overwhelmed by an intense emotion, that of being from the same family, America. I had developed strong love and patriotism for the United States, even before becoming a citizen. I had always been proud to live in this great country; that day, I was going to be part of it.

Once the ceremony was over, the time-consuming process of distributing the certificates took place. The judge would hand a certificate to each of the 400 people. Sitting in the back of the room, I saw row after row of people walking slowly to the judge. I had waited for this moment for years, so an extra minute or even hour seemed like nothing. How many times had I imagined that scene? I had dreamed about it day and night and my dream was becoming reality. Now it was my turn, and my emotions rushed back. I walked calmly to the judge who handed me my certificate. My face broke in a smile; he congratulated me and shook my hand. A photo for some, a handshake for others, or an immense smile, for each there was a special gesture on top of the certificate that we were receiving at last.

My certificate was the irrefutable proof that I was now a citizen. It looked at it as if it were a work of art: it looked like a diploma, adorned with my photo, my name in golden letters and the United States seal in the lower right corner. This "piece of paper" represented for most of us an accomplishment, the end of a journey and at the same time a new beginning. This certificate was like our birth certificate to America.

I admired all our certificates—orderly arranged on yards and yards of table. They held so much life, promises and hopes for future American generations. It was a day of celebration for all! Women and men were cheering. Our long and remarkable journeys were coming to an end on that snowy day in Cleveland. Our destination was one; however, our origins were varied and diverse. From Senegal to China, we all had, in our pursuit of a better life, sacrificed something at one time or another. And even though our stories and paths were unique, that day we were celebrating the common spirit that lives within us -- a spirit of freedom and solidarity that has made the USA strong for hundreds of years.

Outside the room, the mood was definitely happy. People were hugging and kissing each other, and taking many photos. I was watching them, alone, envious of all these people who could share the moment with their families. I looked everywhere, lonely, with tears in my eyes, hoping that one of my loved ones would surprise me by tapping on my shoulder.

I wanted my family to be there with me. I thought about my late grandfather, and how proud he would have been on that day. I also thought about the dire times that my mother had gone through to keep me safe from failure and mediocrity…

Then I felt a twinge in my heart thinking about my sons. I thought especially about El haji who was born in the United States and would never have to go through the many battles I had to fight, the sacrifices, the difficulties encountered, the sleepless nights brightened by a tiny flicker of hope. I was lonely, but happy to think of my sons' brighter future, happy that my descent would contribute to building America and Senegal because they would have a choice. My children now had two cultures, two homelands: they would be able to follow their destiny, pursue their happiness. I had done it, why would they not? Maybe their dreams would materialize in the United States, in Hong Kong, in Dakar, in Sao Paolo, or anywhere I chose to go!

——————————————————————————————

"Today I am a citizen of the United States".

I have lived in this country, as a foreigner, for several years. I got my driver's license, learned English and paid my taxes every year. I had been a permanent resident, waiting impatiently for the completion of the required years before initiating the naturalization procedure. Now that this moment had come, I was experiencing some relief. This emotion, I am sure, was shared by the hundreds of voices who had joined mine in singing during the pledge of allegiance. The same emotion would prompt millions to try and be part of the great American family.

When I travel around the world, I am often asked what it means to be an American citizen, and what it can change in one's life. I always answer in a detailed manner because this allows me to not forget my many obstacles to celebrate my origins and to express my "gratitude" to the land that has adopted me.

Being a citizen of this nation was for me an honor and a privilege. Thousands of people die each year while trying to cross the border to come into the USA. Endless lines of people wait at the door of our embassies around the world, in order to obtain a visa—a visa to dream, a visa to hope. Many will never have the chance to set foot in this great nation and will never taste freedom, or hear the harmonious chords of democracy. And for those who will have found a way to enter illegally and who work tirelessly night and day to merely survive, I know that none of them would try their luck elsewhere in the world. This being said, many Americans forget that they live on a blessed, fertile land where opportunities abound for everyone.

When you are an American citizen, you have the power to create your own story. This ideal comes from the Constitution, which encourages everyone to pursue their happiness. Nothing is given to you. If you have the will, you have the way -- if you are ready to work for it. This will and determination were in me, and America had made the unthinkable become real. One of the fundamental rights of American citizens is to develop their talents, whichever they may be. We are all unique individuals with different talents and the possibility to bloom freely. This mosaic of talents has made America what it is today.

The fundamental rights guaranteed by the American Constitution are illustrated in the "Bill of Rights," the first ten amendments representing the founding principles of this great country. To name a few: freedom of speech, freedom of religion, freedom of the press and the right to assemble. I am proud to be an American and to enjoy principles that I have always aspired to and admired. Here we do not always agree and we have the right to disagree; not only with our family or friends but also with our government and representatives in Congress.

There are many words that can define my understanding of the word "citizenship". But two always come to my mind: opportunity and freedom. What do I mean?

In the USA, I am part of a country that accepted me as an individual, with my small contribution, but not based on my social status or the color of my skin.

I live in a society that favors merit, encourages initiative and respects hard work. This country has let me dream as big as I dare, helped me realize my dreams and share my story around the world.

Opportunity

As an American citizen, the opportunity I refer to differ from the others in so far as it gives access to local and national elections. This civic responsibility lets us play our part in the building of our nation and the world. This opportunity represents the chance to take control of one's destiny.

It is pure self-determination that happens through the American dream. No, it is not a decoy or a legend, since the opportunity to seize it comes every day. This dream comes from an unquenchable thirst to succeed and requires the most enlightening awakening, a sharp and lively mind: this is what makes it unique. It is a dream during which one must stay awake!!

For me, America has been a real land of opportunities enabling me, in spite of my poor background, to chase my dreams freely and therefore to fulfill the needs of my community and mostly of my family. My youth, my social status, my past, the color of my skin, and my lack of experience…everything that could have harmed me elsewhere, made me strong in the United States.

Freedom

I refer here to all the liberties that American citizens enjoy. A freedom for which thousands of Americans have fought over time, relentlessly, sometimes to the point of sacrificing their life.

This valuable freedom is a heritage that must be preserved and respected. Therefore one must never back out, never give in, and never give up: for a "man" who has a free mind can accomplish the unfeasible.

Free, you can settle and develop roots like never before. No one else is controlling your future. Your civic rights and responsibilities are yours to honor. You have the freedom to dream, large or small. It is your dream and yours only.

In search of this dream, I had to lead an incredible fight, complete with sweat and tears. This is how President Theodore Roosevelt's great saying, "Nothing great gets accomplished in this world without hardship, effort and difficulty," became my mantra.

I am sure this mantra also suits my peers who will recognize themselves in the description of our path to naturalization. Even if it had been difficult to wait in never-ending lines, to take endless interviews, to have our fingerprints taken many times over and to undergo numerous "background checks", or to sign many checks to our lawyers and to the government… it was well worth it. We were doing something big. We were becoming American citizens.

"To accomplish something big" is a noble human ambition, and no law in America can forbid millions of individuals to try. The latter share that ambition, with the same fervor and intensity as us Naturalized citizens. In some extreme cases, I think of those who take the risk of illegal immigration, and who live in permanent fear of leaving the country and not being able to come back. Three sad cases come to my mind, showing the difficulty and above all the complexity of being undocumented.

In Senegal, you can find in several families the case of someone who has left and been trapped abroad. A close friend of mine went through this bitter experience. He had agreed from abroad to marry a young Senegalese woman whom he had seen in photos. A quiet wedding took place in his absence, according to the traditional rites.

The marriage was never consummated because for ten years the groom was not able to return to Senegal. He had left with a tourist visa that had already expired. His bride remained faithful to him for ten years, without any physical contact, and ended up requesting a divorce in order to start a new life.

In the United States, being in exile in spite of oneself is also too frequent. I still remember Maria, a Mexican girl whom I met while working at a restaurant called Chevy's. One day she got a call from her native town, and almost immediately dropped the phone… shaky, pale, she fell to the floor and started sobbing. Panic ensued in the restaurant. Maria was simply inconsolable. Ben, the manager, tried to find out what was going on but she could not answer his many questions. Lastly, she explained that her brother had just reported the passing of their mother. Several days before, she had told us about her sadness not to be able to visit her gravely ill mother, back in Mexico. Because she was undocumented, she was condemned to suffer alone, far from her family: she could not leave US soil, since her leaving would have been final. Maria had immigrated to the United States eight years before. She had found a job, to support herself and her family in Mexico. In America, she had married and was hoping to have a baby. But getting this "better" life meant making sacrifices: for eight years, Maria had not been able to see her family, but the little she had was enough to comfort her. Now her mother was no longer alive, her only wish was to drop everything, to leave Chevy's and take the first plane home to see her family. That is what her instinct was urging her to do: attending her mother's funeral would have been Maria's last tribute to her mom. But leaving without the hope of ever returning to America was not an option. She could no longer leave the country that, over the years, had become hers.

The faces, voices, laughs of her people were distant memories. By leaving her country Maria had lost them forever. For her, the American dream was the American trap. The idea of leaving one's family and never seeing them again seemed dreadful to me.

Maria was one of thousands of immigrants who experience this kind of drama every day. There are millions of individuals who want to become legal in order to go back to their original country and see their loved ones.

Years later, during one of my travels in Ohio, as the National Co-Chair of Gen44, I spoke at a rally organized by the Democratic Party during the Obama 2012 campaign. The purpose of the event was to gather the stories of young voters in the city of Cleveland. The most pressing issues were about unemployment, and the most disturbing stories were about immigration.

Tall and thin, 20 year-old Jonathan came dressed in a suit to tell us his story, and send a last cry of despair. When he took the stand, he spoke eloquently, with a firm and calm voice. In spite of his smile, the seriousness on his face showed his sadness. Jonathan explained that he had just been released from jail. He did not look like a criminal but had been convicted, for not being an American citizen. His sentence? 8 months in jail.

Jonathan, who was in the last stage of his deportation process, was going to leave the United States to return to his native country, left when he was two years old. Growing up in Cleveland, Jonathan had no idea that he would one day pay a high price for his parents' illegal presence. But when they were visited at 5:00 am by agents from the immigration services, he realized how desperate their situation was. The agents directed them to go back to their "real" country.

A traumatic experience.

Many youngsters are in the same delicate situation as Jonathan. They are sent back to countries that they know nothing about. Countries that are foreign to them, because they don't speak the language, can't spell or even pronounce the words. Countries whose morals they don't agree with, whose habits they don't understand.

Thousands of young people have been deported that way. Once the patriotic bond with America is untied, their life changes forever and they don't know how to start anew. This is how Jonathan was about to leave everything. The high school, the home, the black jacket to wear at Max's party, (where he would finally tell Kate that he loved her since Kindergarten), the community service job at the local Soup Kitchen… his world, his dreams, his life. He had to leave all that, abruptly, for the unknown, never to come back.

Although his entire life was in the United States, he is not American in the eyes of the law. Which makes me wonder if we are a product of our origins or of our environment?

That morning, in the federal building, my thoughts were with all these people. They are not invisible: you see them every day: at the restaurant, in the bus, in the classrooms.

In Senegal, I already had the seed of hope that America had let me nurture and grow. The source of my Senegalese strength had found its way in America: literally, my family was Senegalese-American. A hybrid family, it had helped me become a responsible, grown-up man. It now felt like I had two parents watching over me, concerned with my well-being and future. I had not felt like an orphan in the past, but on that day I was experiencing the well-deserved confidence that America was granting me. "One people, one purpose, one faith" on the one hand, and "In God we trust" on the other—these two magnificent mottos were mine forever. Oddly, I have to say that they had always been within me. From a tender age, Mam Thione had infused me with this ideal, this line of action.

On that very cold morning in Ohio, in the Carl Stokes federal building in Cleveland, I became a citizen of the United States of America.

That day, I felt compelled to immediately and most efficiently put my talents to work. It was a demonstration of concentrated efforts and overcoming my doubts, hardships and potential. From that moment on, I felt capable of mobilizing all of my energy to serve the community: I had succeeded; others could be inspired to also! With renewed purpose, I geared towards entrepreneurship and the pursuit of the American dream.

CHAPTER XVI

THE DEMOCRATIC PARTY:
A REAL SCHOOL

"Nothing can stand in front of the power of millions of voices calling for change." Barack Obama

One night, I received a call from Congresswoman Shirley Smith, one of the leaders of the Democratic Party in Ohio. She was a candidate in the senatorial elections and offered me to work with her on her campaign, "I need an energetic young person, someone who won't be afraid to swim against the tide. Mayor Franck Jackson doesn't support me, and I think he is close with my opponent. I saw you at work with the mayor, with the youth, and with Kevin Conwell. I like your determination, and I would like to use it for my campaign. What do you think?"

Now resolved to remain selective in the decisions about my political activism, I took a few days to research Shirley and consider her offer. She was well known, she seemed like a sensible person, and the content of her program seemed strong. I decided to support her.

On the suggestion of a few knowing friends, I started working for Shirley Smith as a consultant and campaign director. As the leader of the management of her campaign, I was in charge of campaign strategy, fundraising, and groundwork. This is how I started my agency the Thione Niang Group.

Aware of the immense quantity of work required, Shirley promptly put me to work. My main goal was to increase her visibility among voters and put public opinion on her side. Shirley Smith was senator material, and I really wanted to see her elected. Our fundraising events went very well, but unfortunately our budget remained lean. Therefore, we had to adapt our ambitions to the sobriety of our means and had to devise a strategic approach. I was focused, feeling good, connected, and confident, in spite of the deep pain I felt every time I would let myself slip into thinking about Joy and our son.

The campaign was energetic and magical, because we had a secret weapon: door-to-door canvassing. During long days of hard work, we visited the entire state of Ohio, knocked on every door, and shook thousands of hands relentlessly. Driven by passion and pumped up by pure adrenaline, we no longer slept. It seemed impossible and sometimes even like a huge waste of time.

And this was how we entered the electoral arena and set out to tame the indomitable bull that was our opponent, and would only see red when he looked at us. Our candidate was tireless. She didn't complain once about being fatigued all through her campaigning. She seemed to have wings, and I tried to ingrain this image into the minds of the campaign team members we had recruited: "If your legs no longer carry you, find within yourself the invisible wings that will carry you further. They will always be there for you."

This state of mind perfectly illustrates the expression "mind over body." The expression found life in Shirley, who was a real source of motivation and inspiration for our team. We shared the same energy;

our bond was obvious. I remember people often mistook me for her son because I called her "Mother." We even had the same complexion. Every time someone asked her who I was, she would say, "Yes, yes. Thione is my son." This did not prevent us from disagreeing often— and reaching a compromise was often a challenge.

On election night, our representatives went to the polling places very early. Nervousness and my evening outings had made me tense and sore all over. The feeling of excitement combined with anxiety was a familiar one. Shirley suggested I take a break, but this was inconceivable. "I will have time to sleep after the election," I told her.

During my two previous campaigns, I had developed some helpful tricks, especially in terms of managing the candidates. For example, we would stay up late at night to put up posters and would keep watch until the wee hours of the morning to make sure they would not be taken down. We did that every day until Election Day to make sure that Shirley would stay present in the field.

On Election Day I visited all the polling places to ensure our people were in place. I had to make sure that our candidate's campaign would unfold without any incident. Therefore, I always verified that our teams were in high spirits and motivated at all times. I coordinated all the shuttles for their various transportation needs, and made sure that at lunchtime everyone was catered to. It was like the work of an orchestra conductor.

When the polling places closed, Shirley and I were simply exhausted. Along with her bodyguard, we went to the polling station to monitor our campaign's health. As the results of each town in Ohio became available, we were able to measure the impact of our efforts. Shortly before 3 a.m. I dropped Shirley off at her home so she could rest. But, our campaign was not over and it was impossible to relax on that last day. So, impatient and excited by these last few minutes of suspense, we went back to the polling place to wait for the final results together. When the verdict was announced, we were immensely relieved. The challenge had been met, and Shirley Smith had just been elected a senator of Ohio. We had won!

We had won this election by convincing each voter, one by one, day and night, without any respite. The ten days preceding the election were spent relentlessly prompting people to go vote. This had required enormous determination, but also sincere effort at listening to voters, which helped us make sure that Senator Smith would be a well-informed, as well as authentic, representative.

This victory was Shirley's, of course, but it felt like mine too. My decisions and actions during the campaign had had a positive impact and would influence the futures of every voter. Now that Shirley was a senator, she had a responsibility to better the life of all the people who believed in her. I was moved, thinking that behind every face, every pair of eyes, every handshake, there was no one but a person who had trusted us. In the streets, it was of course Shirley's program that I was explaining, but I was the messenger.. I was a key component of that political machine—a small component, yes, but one who'd had a goal and met it. After being overwhelmed and virtually euphoric, we rapidly gave in to relief and exhaustion. After endless congratulatory hugs with the team, I finally went to sleep. But, as always on election night, the phone didn't stop ringing until the morning.

Phone calls in the morning, in the afternoon, and at night— we had won the election, but the world hadn't stopped turning! I was thrown into a political tornado. During the campaign, I had met many people and had discussed many difficult topics with the greatest possible finesse. Shirley's campaign had been a good omen in regards to the official start of my political work. During the campaign, for example, I had talked to her about my desire to work with young Democrats. I was already an activist at the local level, but I had to better understand how the Democratic Party operated on a larger scale. Shirley had promised to introduce me to the Young Democrats of Ohio.

It was also alongside Shirley that I had one of the most important encounters in my political life. She invited me to Columbus, Ohio, for a meeting that Illinois senator Barack Obama was to attend. As the guest of honor, the young senator had joined all the Democratic leaders to show his support to the party and to Governor Ted Strickland in their fundraising efforts. It was my first major meeting with the Democrats. Shirley was the director of the Black Caucus of Ohio, regrouping the black senators and representatives of the state. When Senator Obama arrived, Smith introduced him to the crowd of about forty representatives and senators. All but three of us were elected officials. It was intoxicating to be among those who had such power within the party, not to mention the emotion I felt upon seeing Barack Obama in person.

Shirley Smith took the microphone, introduced him and said confidently, "Barack, you will be the next president of the United States of America." At the time, Senator Obama had not declared his candidacy. His face showed surprise. I wouldn't be able to say for sure if his surprise was feigned or sincere, but he seemed stirred. He quickly grabbed the mic from Shirley and said calmly, "Don't say that kind of thing. I'm not interested in the presidential election." But Shirley trusted her sixth sense and did not waver, saying, "Thione, this man will be president. You have to be introduced to him!" Shirley had always been very direct, and I really liked this aspect of her personality, though others often loathed it.

Senator Obama did the traditional round of photos and signed his book The Audacity of Hope. He was a very warm person, and I understood then that indeed, that man was going to be the next president of the United States. I was especially impressed by his simplicity and the consideration he had for each person he spoke to. Obama was maintaining, with class and eloquence, the mystery around his own candidacy. He was truly a star within the party. After Shirley, it was my turn to take a photo with him. I shook his hand.

"What is your name?" he asked.

When signing my copy of the book, he misspelled my name and wrote "Sean" instead of "Thione."

"Mister Senator, it is Thione, T-h-i-o-n-e, not Sean."

"Sorry. Your name is special, and so is your accent. Where are you from?"

"From Senegal, in Africa.

"My father is African too, from Kenya."

"Of course, I know that. I read your book!"

He smiled, and then asked me what my role was in the fundraising event so I explained that I was Senator Shirley Smith's campaign director. After a photo and an accolade, he said, "Never forget where you come from. Keep helping your original country." Then he shook my hand and walked over to a group of other senators for a photo. I was incredibly inspired by the fact that this young senator, who everyone was bustling around, also had Africa in his blood. It gave me confidence and showed me that I too would be able to make a difference and make a significant contribution to working on issues that were important to me—not only in Ohio, but nationally and internationally as well.

After the photo shoot, the senator gave an electrifying speech to boost the spirits of Democratic supporters in Ohio. He encouraged us to fight for our ideas because they were, in his view, what define us best. "By fighting for our ideas, we will get our candidates elected," he said before leaving. It was then that I realized just how critical Ohio is to presidential candidates.

During the reception, contacts were made and business cards were exchanged freely. I was talking to local leaders when Shirley came over to introduce me to Sarah, president of the Young Democrats of Ohio. Sarah expressed how happy she was to broaden, through my participation, the ranks of the Youth of the Democratic Party. A few days later she recommended me to Troy, the president of the Young Democrats in Cuyahoga County.

Sarah had told me that at the national level, the party's youth held four meetings per year, with the next meeting the following month. Each state would report on the status of the party and its level of mobilization within that state. During that meeting, scheduled for mid-November, sixteen people were to represent Ohio. I volunteered to be a representative at the meeting.

One week before Thanksgiving, I went to Philadelphia with the Young Democrats of Ohio delegation. The sessions were held at the Doubletree Hotel; there were people everywhere. In the presence of so much youth, so much energy, so much drive, I was like a fish in water. I value young people for what they embody, the ability and desire to progress towards the future.

At the meeting, everybody knew each other so well that the whole scene looked like a family reunion. I was the newcomer, and I felt foreign to the situation. Intrigued and slightly disoriented, I asked Sarah, "How do they all know each other?"

"It's easy, all you need is assiduity. Don't worry. Three meetings and you will know everyone," she said in a reassuring voice.

In her opening speech, the national president of the Young Democrats announced that the party intended to create a group of college activists called the College Caucus. This group was going to have an executive board and there would be "special" elections to fill the president, vice president, secretary, and treasurer positions. And although this meeting was scheduled to last four days, we were only two days away from the special election! My activist's instinct reacted immediately to this unexpected announcement.

At the end of the meeting, I went to the members of the Ohio delegation to introduce myself. "I will be candidate to these elections. I want to be part of the board of the College Caucus. In fact, I want to be president of the College Caucus," I said very seriously. In response, there was an avalanche of mocking, amused, and coarse laughs. The laughter wasn't meant to be cruel—they believed they were being realistic. The delegation members laughed happily and openly, and it was only when they noticed that I was not laughing that they realized my intentions were sincere. With a serious look on my face, I watched them in silence.

"So, this isn't a joke?" asked a young man clad in navy blue.

"Politics is a serious matter, and I am a serious person," I said, looking him straight in the eye.

"But nobody knows you! You just arrived and you want to be president? No one will vote for you. You are going to be ridiculed!"

My conviction didn't sway. "I will be a candidate," I said, regardless of what my party comrades thought, although I'd thought they would be more supportive.

"In an election you always win something: either notoriety, or experience, or both," often said Reggie Maxton.

I will run, and I will win, I thought. And euphoria swept over me as if I had already won. In my mind, there was no outcome other than victory, but faced with reluctance from my own side regarding my campaign, I had to gather other allies. Fortuitously I met a man from Florida who seemed well connected to the majority of the members. His name was Omar Khan, and he was a talented young Democrat. He was originally from Pakistan, and we both shared a desire to see minorities play a bigger role within the party. The day after we met, and every day until the election, we spent our time convincing people to join our platform, which was to rally young Democrats across the country with the objective of the 2008 presidential election. Obtaining their support was no easy task, as support was articulated along geographic lines.

On the day of the vote, three candidates were on the starting line: Arkansas, New York, and Ohio, which I represented. A few minutes before the vote, each candidate was asked to make a two-to-five-minute speech, explaining the reason why he or she deserved to be elected president. The candidate from Arkansas was so fascinatingly eloquent that I was tempted to give him my vote! Speaking in public seemed to be easy for him, and it was clear he enjoyed it a lot. The candidate from New York was also remarkable. After ten short minutes, it was my turn. My desire was intact, but was I going to be on par with the previous speakers? I dug from the bottom of my heart to summon the necessary energy and determination to convey my ideas to the audience. My speech highlighted the fact that minorities within the Democratic Party were missing from party leadership in spite of their involvement and support. I called their attention to the fact that this reality could cost us voters, especially in areas where minorities live. As a matter of fact, women and ethnic minorities were at the heart of my concern.

"All Americans should be represented by our party. My dear friends, we are currently facing a choice that will define the future of our party. The choice is ours: either we stop being a discreet and discriminatory group, closed to the little people, or we open wide the doors of our common house, the Democratic Party, to welcome all those who share with us the desire to live in a great America, fostering peace, cohesion, and prosperity. It is the latter option, I think, that will bring the party the lifeblood required for growing. The College Caucus is the future of the Democratic Party and the future of the United States. On this day we bear the heavy responsibility of deciding for our people; let's choose wisdom. Let's accept the extended hand of the minorities who support our principles unconditionally. Let's move our party in the direction of the American people."

In spite of the ovation that followed my speech, the candidate from Arkansas was elected president. It greatly surprised my delegation, but I received a vote of confidence from the voters and became vice president. Stephanie became secretary. I didn't know it yet, but eight months later Luther Lowe, the elected president, would resign and I would become president of the National College Caucus of the Young Democrats of America.

Back in Cleveland, the news of my election created a real buzz. Councilmember Conwell congratulated me and published a press release saluting the election of "a son of Cleveland" at the national level. I was honored in the meeting room at the town hall, that same room where, one year earlier, I had been an outcast.

Following the election of Shirley Smith, and as part of her senatorial swearing-in, there was a big party with important people such as the governor and lieutenant governor of Ohio, as well as mayors of various cities in the state. Among the guests was Stephanie Tubbs Jones, delegate of the 11th Congressional District representing Ohio in Washington. The cream of the crop of was there. Shirley had asked me to talk on behalf of the state youth. I noticed that out of the 200 guests attending, only three were in their thirties.

The audience found my speech relevant and approved of my wish to work so young people could have real opportunities, enabling them to acquire the experience necessary to better serve their communities. From then on, I became a known speaker, sometimes even consulted, on all matters related to youth and their involvement in the party. Among the new contacts I established that evening were two men with fascinating records: the previous delegate Louis Stokes and Samuel Tidmore.

Louis Stokes was from a poor family from the suburbs of Cleveland. In spite of his lack of means, he had managed to overcome his condition to become the first black congressman from Ohio, as well as a cofounder of the Congressional Black Caucus. His younger brother, Karl Stokes, was one of the first black mayors of Cleveland.

Samuel Tidmore, Mr. Stokes's right-hand man and director of a television station, talked to me about his commitment alongside the Reverend Martin Luther King, Jr. and Jesse Jackson. He had been the director of the "rainbow coalition" which had fought for equal rights, regardless of race. In my view, these two men were role models of success and perseverance, and I deeply admired them. Tidmore even became a mentor for me. His strength of character was a real source of inspiration, and he was blessed with an exceptional gift for listening, especially to young people. At the time, he was recruiting many young people to work at his television station or in the McDonald's restaurants he owned, providing each one with an opportunity. He was a kind of social entrepreneur, who never feared that his business success would suffer from his generosity. His former career as a professional football player had taught him perseverance, determination, diligence, and sacrifice. That was his message to the young population. That was the precious gift he gave me.

During that same reception, a new opportunity arose. One of the top executives within Cuyahoga County was a Harvard Law School graduate named Peter Lawson Jones. He expressed his interest in me managing his re-election campaign. He was a hard worker with superior intelligence. I accepted his offer a year later.

Meanwhile, I had been promoted to that position of treasurer of the Young Democrats in Cuyahoga County after the standing treasurer resigned. In January 2007, I organized support to run to be vice president of Cuyahoga at the local level. One night, I got a call from a friend, asking if I would go vote the next day. I knew nothing about that vote, but understood that this was an attempted exclusion by some party members in order to steal positions. I responded, saying I'd be there.

The following day, I went to the Democratic Party's local headquarters in Cuyahoga County. There were two groups: on the one side was the group I was serving, which had not alerted me, and on the other side the opposing clan, whose people explained that a "hold-up" was being organized clandestinely. The opposing side explained that given my experience as a campaign manager for various candidates, and my ability to defend my beliefs, I could jump sides and they would support me to win the presidency. They already had candidates for the posts of vice president and treasurer.

We all belonged to the same family, sharing the same values and beliefs. We were all Democrats. Their offer fueled my motivation to carry out my ideas and my candidacy, and I promised to broaden our small organization of young people and to make it an example for the party. We had to break free of our clan-like patterns in order to become a winning force.

Laden with all these beliefs, I became the president of Cuyahoga County Young Democrats, against the will of my political opponents, and thanks to my allies, who then tried to control me during my entire mandate. I worked to rally thousands of young people to the organization, and because their support gave credibility to my proposals for strengthening the party, the legitimacy of my leadership role was reinforced.

In my work, I was paying special attention to women and black and Hispanic minorities, which didn't please everyone. However, I managed to establish the bases of the organization in Cuyahoga County's fifty-five towns. Within those towns we had identified young people who could represent us and relay the expectations and grievances of the population. We had a real part to play with the elected officials, who found in our melting pot a great source of votes. The fundraising was remarkable. In Cleveland we hosted the Young Democrats of Ohio's annual meeting, as I had represented Cleveland and Ohio at the national level. In addition to being president of the Young Democrats of Cuyahoga County, I was also the president of the College Caucus at the national level. I did not want to stop; I could not stop.

Every two years, Young Democrats organize a national convention to energize the whole party. In 2009, the YD national office appointed me president in charge of international affairs. My role was to broaden the influence of the party throughout the world. We had a rather modest network in place, but our vision was to expand it to the entire world. So it followed that I was tasked with representing the YD on all continents. As a group, we actively promoted important values such as peace, democracy, tolerance, and community involvement in various countries of the world.

I took baby steps. Over time, I increasingly understood politics. I observed, listened, analyzed, and reflected a lot during these first experiences. My efforts were enhanced by teamwork, which proved to be greatly motivating and enriching. We worked relentlessly! Again, I dared to seize opportunities; preparing myself for the next phase at every chance it was possible. Meeting Barack Obama forever forged my political identity with the Democrats. His extraordinary charisma made an impression on me; it was a key stage in my life as a young Senegalese-American. Who would have imagined this as possible if I had not maintained a spark of hope?

CHAPTER XVII

YES, WE CAN!
(2007-2008)

"Do not go where the path may lead. Go where there is no path and leave a trail." Ralph Waldo Emerson

While Hillary Clinton, Joe Biden, and John Edwards had already confirmed their candidacies, Senator Barack Obama had not. America was thirsty for a new era, and the people, including the media, were wondering who the next president of the United States would be.

Each candidate was furbishing his or her arguments, and the vigil had already started in some circles. This is how Senator John Edwards came to be seen as the candidate with the best solutions to fight poverty. Hillary Clinton was deemed the logical heir to a party that her husband had helped build. She was supposedly undefeatable and according to her supporters, the primaries were already won. Joe Biden, a high-flying senator, would re-establish America in the esteem of the world at a time when the federal government was being criticized for the Iraq War and the American military presence in Afghanistan. Although the battle of ideas had already begun, Obama was not officially in the race. I was among the people who foresaw his candidacy.

"Obama has a personality that inspires trust. He's got natural leadership," I told my friends. My contacts, a majority of who were more experienced than me, would laugh, saying, "You don't get it. Obama is not ready."

Even my friend Reggie Maxton would not believe it.

"At all the meetings I attended, I saw Bill Clinton support Democratic candidates at various levels. It's obvious he will support his wife. It will be Hillary against the Republicans," Maxton would often say.

"In any case, Barack Obama doesn't sound too good! "Barack" sounds Muslim and Arabic—what a combination! And where does "Obama" come from? With a name like that, he doesn't stand a chance. The memories from nine-eleven are still too vivid," said one person.

"Where did you get this idea? Obama is black. America won't elect a black president for another fifty years!" exclaimed another.

Each explained his reasoning. Even the pastor Jesse Jackson, a leader in civil rights activism and the first black candidate in US primaries, was not in favor of Obama, telling me, "You believe in Obama because you come from Africa and you have only a partial knowledge of the political ideas that define America."

Many thought I was uneducated and naive. These heated discussions would often leave me feeling knocked out, like a Senegalese wrestler exiting the arena. I was exhausted, and the primaries had not even started.

Sometimes I wondered how people around me could be so blind about Barack Obama.

I had had the opportunity of seeing him interact with people, work on the ground, and give speeches—and I believed that this man had an untapped potential that could help America. While the international reputation of the largest global power was on the decline and social problems were mounting domestically, I believed Obama was the best candidate for re-energizing international leadership and the sense of humanity that defined America.

With low labor costs in foreign factories, many American companies were reaping the benefits of foreign outsourcing. This is why hundreds of jobs were shipped to China, India, and other countries. It was critical to renew hope among the increasingly worried middle class. Indeed, America was not spared the effects of the global economic crisis. In every household, daily hardship was more and more noticeable and the downturn spared no one. Even my family in Senegal was requesting more money to face the increasing cost of living. Unemployment and inflation were the two curses weighing painfully on the entire world. The crisis was developing without any remedy, spreading fear and despair.

For me, Obama embodied the answer to this painful situation. I had faith in him and in the hope he was inspiring. I thought he would be able to meet the challenges that America was facing. But at that point, I could only hope that he would declare his candidacy. Therefore, I was very happy to hear that he would announce his candidacy in Springfield, Illinois. Was it time to stop praying and roll up our sleeves?

Upon hearing this news, a voice inside me said that this would be an historic moment for America and for the world. I bought a ticket to Springfield—I had to see for myself why Obama was so inspiring. I needed to know the candidate I trusted better. On an icy morning, wrapped in thick coats, we sat on the steps of Springfield's Old State Capitol, where in 1858, Abraham Lincoln gave his famous speech "House Divided." We were cold, but our hearts were warm. We were only a small group compared to the rest of America, but we we had the energy of a very large group given the size of our conviction. We were waiting for Obama to arrive at the Springfield Town Square. We were not there by chance, and I knew that this day would be part of a great and historic story. The senator came, clad in a black coat and a red tie, with his wife Michelle Obama, their two daughters, and a big smile.

His speech was eloquent. He talked about his concern for America who, according to him, "had to rise with honor," and added that it was that concern that had prompted him to enter the race. Listening to Obama, I whispered without realizing it, "It would be long and exciting." The person sitting next to me agreed.

I remain convinced that none of us left Springfield that day without the absolute trust that Obama was the person the country needed. Our belief, however, didn't stop Hillary's rise in the polls. Feminist organizations were mobilizing around her and black leaders, almost all close to Bill Clinton like Jesse Jackson, were pushing African-American people to support the Democratic hopeful. Black members of Congress, such as John Louis—a Georgia Democrat who had fought alongside Martin Luther King, Jr.—were also behind Hillary. This was very surprising! Most of them said that they could not support a candidate for the sole reason he had the same complexion as they did. However, for his supporters, Obama was not only black. Why should a man's identity be boiled down to only his skin color? Barack Obama is from America, from Africa, from Asia, from Europe, from Oceania. He is the world. Obama was the solution.

Back in Cleveland, I was organizing with friends who wanted to help Obama conquer the White House. Under our initiative, a fundraiser took place on February 26, 2007, at the Marriott Hotel a few days after his announcement in Springfield, which Obama attended with his special assistant Reggie Love. Afterwards we held a parade on the Cuyahoga County College campus in Cleveland, with 5,000 people attending.

Three days later, like every Monday, I was at the town hall meeting. The most influential leader in the county, delegate Stephanie Tubbs Jones, was a good friend of the Clintons and was leaning in favor of Hillary. As a matter of fact, Bill was the godfather of Marvin, Jones's son. Furthermore, Jones was copresident of Hillary's campaign. She really mastered the geopolitics of Ohio, and most of the elected officials in Cuyahoga County were her protégés. Therefore it surprised no one that the governor of Ohio, too, was in favor of Hillary.

The quest for votes in Ohio was organized very precisely. I began to fully understand the very strategic nature of the state. It was a special state in the sense that no Republican had ever been able to win the White House without winning in Ohio.

The political support of young voters, and especially of young Democrats, was very important to candidates. The youth were mobilized to give a speech explaining their vision of the future, which took place during a large conference at the Hilton Hotel in Washington, D.C. This event mostly benefited Clinton and Edwards. To reinforce the presence of people in our camp, we had written on our signs, "Obama Volunteers." A young organizer, Shaney Whitaker, and I were hard at work, but people were not exactly flocking to our table.

That day, we saw that the room where our candidate would speak was mostly filled with supporters of the opposing camps. When Hillary Clinton ended her speech, what we'd feared would happen did. A thunder of applause confirmed the hegemony of the Clintons on the Democratic Party. With pessimistic hearts and nervous legs, we stood up to welcome our candidate when his turn came. The faith we had in Obama was our energy source. Far from being defeatists, we understood that we would have to work even harder to materialize the dream of seeing Obama at the helm of the country's government. Although it is true that power goes to whomever wants it most, it is also true that one must learn not only to desire power, but then to conquer it.

Therefore, one month later, we did not hesitate to go to Chicago to attend an initiative called Camp Obama. Camp Obama was a sort of pre-campaign university and training program. Thanks to that training we becoming more and more familiar with Obama, and learned about his vision, his ideas, his assets, and his vulnerabilities. We also studied voters psychology and reporters' traps. By the end of the program, we were ready. All the more so because our "coach" was no other than Barack Obama's own mentor in community organizing, Gerald Kellman. We were a family, although all different from one another. With the intent of bonding together, our mentor asked each of us to express our reasons for supporting Obama. I explained that the commitment for me was also personal, because I wanted my American-born son to grow up in a better country than the US had been during George W. Bush Jr.'s administration. Although America had been on the decline, I believed Obama would give us leverage to help us rise again. However, Senator Obama didn't hide that he knew what his opponents were saying: that he had no chance.

This motivated us to make a difference in Iowa, the first state on the primaries schedule. For Obama, a victory in Iowa would ripple into other states. After the training sessions, I divided my time between Ohio and Chicago, bringing all my resources to the campaign. Several months later, I accepted a community organizer position with the Obama campaign. First in Cincinnati and then in Cleveland, I organized the mobilization.

My position in the Young Democrats, both locally and nationally, helped me get regular feedback regarding the trends and changes in opinion within the party. We would mostly manage differences in the orientations to give our entity, since each primary candidate had his or her own lobbying activities within the Young Democrats. However we all had to keep in mind our common objective: elect a Democrat for president of the United States.

On the evening of January 3, 2008, the Iowa results were announced: Obama was leading, followed first by Edwards and then Clinton. Barack Obama's speech created a surge in confidence, an encouragement for his supporters who shouted, "Yes, we can!" He said that no one could stop millions of people who were determined to create their own destinies. The victory in Iowa helped strengthen our ranks. Most of those who had turned their backs on us rushed to the Obama camp, saying the candidate's words and ideas would reverse the trends. Iowa confirmed that Obama was a legitimate candidate. At last!

This reversal rippled and reached even my friend councilmember Kevin Conwell. An ex-supporter of Hillary, he joined our ranks four days after the results and spoke eloquently about Senator Obama during a TV interview on MSNBC. At the council members meeting in Cleveland, some members were upfront about their support, and others wished to meet the senator. Attacks from opponents, especially those supporting Clinton, were bitter and sufficiently strong to prove that Obama had become a very serious candidate.

This is how the battle really started. Two weeks later, it was uncertain Obama would keep his advantage in New Hampshire. All the media were there, as well as campaign managers. Unfortunately we lost, since the results were in favor of Clinton. We Obama supporters commented that "She had won thanks to the tears shed on TV while explaining her dream for America" the day after the Iowa results.

There was a non-stop back-and-forth between the two camps. A political transhumance took place in favor of Hillary. The competition was on again. We adapted the mobilizing efforts to each state: North Carolina, South Carolina, and Nevada. Then on March 4, a day called "Super Tuesday," all major states held their primary elections. The results were not bad for our camp, but there was one cloud overshadowing the picture: we had lost Ohio.

In North Carolina, Obama's speech was a call for people to unite beyond their differences and to promote change. That goal could only be reached if middle class, the base of the population pyramid, were really mobilized. This speech by the Senator was a real success and made him a leader worthy of America. However, within his own party, the division was reaching ever more worrisome proportions. Some super delegates had not decided between Obama and Hillary, and the back-and-forth between the two camps was higher than ever. We feared for the party cohesion. In one of his speeches, Bill Clinton had linked Obama's victory in South Carolina to the heavily black demographics over there.

The former president had to distance himself from the campaign, which brought a little serenity to our camp. All along the campaign, Bill Clinton had lobbied for his wife, but without creating any significant advantage. Now the head-on buckling with the Clinton duo was no longer needed. From then on we had only one opponent, but still a fearsome opponent because Hillary had won important states and remained a candidate until the Democrat convention in August. But one less piece on the chessboard meant an increased chance for Obama to become the Democratic Party's candidate.

Two months before the convention, the Republican opponent John McCain had a good lead over a Democratic Party embattled in endless rivalries. In order to speed up the selection process, some suggested that Hillary accept the nomination of vice president. I was in favor of that option, as I said to the Cleveland press. Just before the convention, other dominos tumbled. More super delegates joined our camp and brought a little confidence that the party would be united.

The Democratic National Convention

In August, the long-awaited Democratic Convention was held over a period of three days in Denver, Colorado. Some thought that Obama would not win, while others threatened to vote for McCain if Obama won the primaries. After the designation of Obama as the Democratic candidate, I was surprised that Biden was chosen as a vice presidential candidate. How could a man who had so openly criticized Obama become such an ardent supporter of his ideas? There was more shake than harm among the Democrats. Bill and Hillary Clinton declared their support. All parties worked hard to heal the wounds from the long primaries battle.

Republican John McCain had a beautiful past of a loyal American patriot. He was a war veteran and a senator, and he had more than thirty years of career experience. The mobilization around Obama didn't leave room for improvisation. The guidelines took into account the new technologies such as social media and Internet, which became highly strategic in this campaign. Our team was foreseeing enough to master these tools, minimally used by the opponent. As a matter of fact, Obama spent $26 million on new technologies versus only $3.6 million by McCain.

Both camps openly courted young voters, the Holy Grail of this election. For this conquest, we had two great weapons: music and sports. Luckily for us, rapper Jay-Z and basketball player LeBron James were both Democrats. A series of concerts was launched by Jay-Z with LeBron James attending. The target was the "swing states," which could at any time go to one candidate or the other. The challenge for us was to mobilize our troops of voters so that they would show their support at the ballot. Thanks to these two iconic figures in American pop culture, we had to register as many young people as possible on the voter lists.

Our strategy was that of business marketing. In order to get a concert ticket, you had to show your voter's identification card. It was a first in the United States, and Cleveland became the first town to benefit from this innovation. Jay-Z and LeBron James prompted young people to vote so they could decide for themselves what their future would be. We had to work twice as hard in Cuyahoga to avoid losing all of Ohio because we had a strong Democratic concentration in the county. Three months before the general election, I was in Cincinnati working as a community organizer. These were rough times, because my arguments were not well received in the mostly Republican neighborhoods.

In Cincinnati, I met very two interesting people, Tim and Marie. These two volunteers hosted me for the six months I spent in the state. Tim was a writer and a literature teacher at Xavier University. They were white, older Democrats, both from traditional Republican families. Some members of their families were downright racist. Tim and Marie were very religious and I would often go to church with them. Because a church is the house of God, it didn't bother me as a Muslim.

Tim and Marie had a rare quality in that they really loved people. They practiced their faith with honesty and in their every action. They were good, open, considerate, attentive, and especially sincere.

One Sunday, after church, they invited their parents for dinner at their home. "They don't like black people," said an embarrassed Tim. I joked to ease the tension but I later realized that that had been a mild way to put it: to put it bluntly, their parents hated blacks.

The questions they asked were the ones I had expected, and revolved around my origins, my work, and the reason for my presence in Cincinnati. When they found out I was working for the Obama campaign, Marie's brother blurted out, "Why Obama? Because he is black like you?"

Tim tried to come to my rescue, but I answered, "You are right to ask this question, even American blacks have asked me that. It is true that Obama is not white, but he is not black either. He is the person symbolizing the best of America today and for tomorrow. Obama is the future."

With a smirk, he answered, "I support McCain. Obama means nothing to me. There is no chance I will vote for him."

"You vote for whoever you please, but I think Obama is the best candidate."

"You are stupid to support Obama,"

I was used to this kind of talk. Eager to change the topic, Marie showed us photos of children. We ate and talked without discussing any more politics. As a community organizer, I worked from 7 a.m. till 1 a.m., Monday through Saturday. On Sundays, we would go to church. My schedule was tightly packed!

I had noticed a real change among the political activists. They would gather together some money to pay expenses, and those that could not contribute financially would lend their house and host other visiting supporters. The personal involvement of all was palpable.

I was fascinated by these efforts, because in Africa it is very different. In Senegal, a bodyguard, who carries a briefcase full of cash often accompanies a campaigning candidate. Yes, ethical concerns have made those briefcases more discreet, but in practice things have not improved. Candidates give money to try to buy the consciences and the votes.

Numerous anecdotes illustrate this point in each country. In Benin, a member of Give1Project told me a well-known fact. A candidate to the presidential election had visited a village to express his views on his principles and his vision for the country. While he was about to say good-bye to the people without having given them anything, he decided to take the pulse of a few people in the audience. A young man raised his hand, asking to be heard: "I think your politics are very slow! Your brother from the other party came by three days ago and gave us money. You came to talk about the country, but what do you bring for us individually? Nothing!"

The ballots revealed that the candidate with the "slow politics" lost the election.

In the Obama campaign, I earned a second grandmother. Mrs. Watson was a big-hearted woman, who often brought me food, saying, "You are not eating, Thione. You are skinny." In addition to being a great cook, Mrs. Watson was a rugged activist, fully devoted to the ideas of the Obama camp. She was one of the most effective local coordinators. Every day, we had to log a significant number of registrations onto the electoral lists. I trained other team members in the art of addressing young people in the tough neighborhoods, whose hopes and expectations I could relate to.

Mrs. Watson was popular among those in her parish. She had no trouble negotiating a few minutes for a political speech for me in front of the members of her church. The speech earned us a few volunteers, who at the end of the service expressed their desire to help bring America behind Obama. They had a real drive to turn a page and design their future the way our candidate wanted them to be able to. In the entire country, this wish had become an extraordinary movement, bursting with energy; it had grown beyond all hopes only three months before the election. I already knew that it was a movement that would make history in the country. I knew that one day, it would be discussed the way we talk today about the unification of the North and South after the Civil War.

Mrs. Watson was extremely generous. She knew that I loved sweet tea and soul food, and would bring me some every week. Since she was from Georgia, renowned for its sweet tea, I was in good hands. Her spontaneity reminded me of the grandmothers in Senegal, a country nicknamed Téranga for the generosity and hospitality of its population.

Mrs. Watson had introduced me in her family as her grandson. Her husband and children had welcomed me like the latest member of the family. Every time I would go back to Cleveland, Mrs. Watson and I would speak on the phone. Two months before the election, I got a message on my voicemail. It was from M. James Watson.

"Your American grandmother is in a difficult medical condition." This piece of news sent me in a panic. I tried to reach him all day, to no avail. At night, M. Watson was at last able to answer my call and gave me the horrible news. "Your American grandmother passed away—heart attack."

The passing of my American grandmother taught me that nothing is forever in this world, and that it is important to love people because they can leave us at any time. On the morning of the funeral, I went from Cleveland to Cincinnati in the church that she usually attended. It was the first time I attended a funeral where the deceased is exposed for everyone to see; there is no such practice in the Muslim religion. When it was my turn to bow in front of the body, I was struck by the serene look on her face. She was sleeping, after a life filled with commitment and dedication. Her husband James introduced me as a young man, a grandson that had occupied a special place in his wife's heart, saying, "She even cried when Thione went back to Cleveland."

Per James's request, I had the privilege of expressing, in front of all, the sorrow of having lost a grandmother and a partner in battle. My homage was brief and difficult. I will always keep this exceptional family in my heart. I went back to Cleveland even more fired up.

Obama was favorably viewed in the polls. We were just a few days away from the election. Just before the last debate between Obama and McCain, I proposed to organize a debate between young Democrats and young Republicans in Cuyahoga. That event was to be a place for freedom of speech, and an opportunity to reaffirm Obama's ideas, which were becoming more and more popular with the American people. Some friends thought that this was risky, because Republicans and Democrats often avoided each other. It was a sensitive issue and some thought that the Republicans would oppose the idea.

I invited Joe to lunch to test his reaction to the idea. As the president of the Young Republicans in Cuyahoga County, Joe was a very conservative Republican, but he also was very open-minded. After our talk, he expressed his agreement in principle and offered to run the idea by his friends.

The moderator of the debate had to have a neutral stance. Terry Travis, president of a non-partisan youth organization, was perfect for the role. The debate took place and yielded many intense moments, exchanges of ideas, and presentations of visions between the two camps—two camps shared the common objective of building a bigger, safer, wealthier, more just America. The event, held in the conference center in downtown Cleveland, reported high attendance. One hour later, Obama and McCain were facing America one more time for their last big debate.

Two days before the election, Barak Obama had gone on his last round of local meetings all over the United States. Large cities and the swing states were his campaign's highest priority. In Ohio, where I was leading the Young Democrats, Obama visited Cleveland on the last day. Mobilization was at its peak, in spite of November's cold weather. Obama brought along his daughters Sasha and Malia, David Axelrod, David Plouff, and Reggie Love, his ever-present assistant. Bruce Springsteen, rock star and Obama supporter, had come to sing at the opening of the meeting.

The senator had lost his maternal grandmother the day before. This event saddened all of America. Once introduced, Obama ran over to the lectern and took the microphone. The ovations were deafening. He paused to thank the crowd with an irresistible smile, as he eased into his speech.

He said he had seen the best and the worst over the last few days. He mentioned his joy, having spoken with the young and the old, manufacturers, business people, and workers, thanks to whom a small movement becomes a huge trend. He spoke about the pain he felt, brought on by his grandmother's death the day before.

"My grandmother, who fought so that today I have my place in the American dream, is no longer," he said. In tears, he paused. I too cried, thinking about my grandfather. In spite of having moved the entire crowd, Obama could not alleviate his pain even in this time of intense communion with the people. When he burst into tears in front of over 80,000 supporters, the crowd chanted, "Yes, we can!"

Obama spoke of the need to for America to get a new pilot. To offer the country an opportunity to remain the most respected country on earth. To work so that the land that best represents fundamental values of equality and opportunity can improve the rest of the world.

Al the efforts of the past few months were to be judged in the forty-eight hours following. All night, the campaign headquarters held a vigil. Logistical questions were closely examined. Volunteer lawyers were mobilized to supervise the voting process. It was an all-nighter.

The next day felt too short to carry out everything that had to be accomplished. The election included races for senators, council members, and the mayor. But the real issue at stake was the election of the next leader of the most important country in the world.

As the president of the Young Democrats, I received an invitation to a radio talk show to discuss the importance of young people going to vote. Bashir Jones, at the time the youngest radio host on Radio One, interviewed me along with a panel of Republican and Democrat leaders. A phone call interrupted the show. The producer was waving frantically behind the glass wall to alert us. It was Senator Obama. Radio One is a leading hip-hop venue and it was no coincidence that the candidate chose this medium to urge young Americans to go out and vote. Obama greeted us, and then congratulated us for the energy we were investing in the campaign.

All day, I visited polling places with other campaign team members to locate and solve potential problems. At 7:30 p.m. came the moment of truth. The closing of polling places had launched the countdown to the name of the new American president. The initial results showed the two camps were even. Stress and nervousness were at their peak.

We had organized a watching event at the Hyatt in Cleveland. Hundreds of people were there. Little by little, results came in. And at 1:30 a.m., CNN anchor Wolf Blitzer announced the victory of the senator from Illinois. Barack Obama was elected forty-fourth president of the United States! Everyone burst into tears. I thought of this new America, of future generations, and of Mrs. Watson. But I also thought of the challenges stemming from the new responsibility to build a better country with a new leader. I gave a few interviews under the light of the cameras. It was a light-filled moment indeed, a light that never left me.

Despite very different backgrounds, teams of volunteers worked together campaigning for Obama. Diversity proved to be a strength and an asset. Throughout the campaign, I met extraordinary people who left an impression on me for life. The diversity of ages and ethnicities, difference in lifestyle, and the varied experiences that all these people brought toward a single goal—the victory of Barack Obama—made me think about the expression, "unity is strength." I believe I have never lived it (life) with such intensity since.

CHAPTER XVIII

ENGAGE IN GENEROUS
PROJECTS: GIVE1PROJECT

"Life's most persistent and urgent question is what are you doing for others?" Dr. Martin Luther King Jr.

The day after his inauguration in January 2009, Barack Obama gathered all his campaign staff, regardless of their rank. All the teams who had worked on the campaign were invited to a ball. This joyful event was one of a series of parties where people cheered, talked, or simply listened to music and danced happily. All the people who had contributed to the campaign were invited: Geniuses of internet mobilization as well as artists such as Jay-Z, Beyoncé or Will.i.am. Exhaustion was ever-present although everyone was truly happy. The president called our attention on the energy we had invested in the campaign, and spoke of the need to transform this energy in a source of progress for the community. He urged us to keep up the flame that had lived in us and motivated us during the entire campaign.

"Don't let this energy die", he said. "My victory is the irrefutable proof that in the end your energy is « palpable ». I was elected despite the odds. We showed the entire world that we can do it. Keep that flame that is in each of you. You can achieve what you have always dreamed of. Don't let this energy die, don't let this flame dwindle."

Suggesting several action plans, he offered us to serve near him in Washington to deliver on the promises, or to serve within our communities, or, why not… to serve internationally and to share a piece of this formidable energy to accompany thousands of people in their quest for a fruitful and wealthy future. Without any apolitical affiliation, this message was universal. His latest suggestion inspired me, and I realized that this was what I wanted to do. It seemed possible and essential to spend my life serving innovative ideas. So, like Lavoisier had demonstrated, nothing would be lost, nothing would be created, everything would be transformed. The energy used during the electoral battle would not dissipate, but would take another form.

From then on, I overflowed with inspiration. I remembered my difficult start in life in Kaolack, while right then I was sitting in the same room with the most powerful man in the world. I realized how lucky I was to be there, and vowed to help other young people around the world make their dream happen. But for that, they had to nurture and respect their dream, then commit and move forward. This is how Give1Project was born, on the night of this luminous encounter with Obama.

Not long before the creation of Give1Project, I was still working in my favorite field, the promotion of young people. Marcia Fudge, Congresswoman in Ohio and then-current president of the

Congressional Black Caucus, had asked me to work on the youth issues. In charge of the education, civil society and employment policies, I would regularly travel between the two cities. I had accepted her offer, and was working with her to materialize her vision for the youth. As a matter of fact, I created for her a « Leader's Program », an initiative that consisted in selecting every year the most promising ten leaders of Ohio to reward them and provide America with role-models. This would entice the young people to stay in the state and continue working for its development.

Thanks to this experience in Congress, I learned the works about this prestigious institution. I also better understood institutional America through the mechanisms for creating laws and amendments. While being in Congress, I worked to develop both Give1Project and Thione Niang Group, a consulting firm in communication and political mobilization. After one year of hard workdays in Congress and nights building Give1Project, I decided to leave everything to travel around the world and focus only on Give1Project. We are now present on five continents, and make up the five fingers of a hand that every day, works on creating better futures.

Give1Project wants to throw bridges between the youths of the world. I have uninterruptedly given speeches all over the world and measured the need for knowledge and action felt by my peers. In that mission, I have been lucky to meet reliable partners with a huge impact on their era and a great vision for their kind. Together we created a new spirit for the young people. Although their horizon should be the blue color of hope, it is often grey and laden with stormy clouds. With these illustrious leaders, we lend a hand to the future. It is an everyday, everywhere, everyone mission.

In 2012, I received an invitation in Senegal to preside over the ceremony of English Lovers Awards, a national recognition of the most eloquent in English students. I remembered with emotion the English Club from my teenage years. What would my life be if I hadn't belonged in that club? Of little importance and often seen as entertaining only, the English Club had been a lucky break, a blessing that opened the doors of the world for me, although I was only from Kaolack.

During the ceremony, I had to deliver a speech on leadership. At meeting time, an immense crowd had gathered in front of the théâtre Sorano. This event was important for many people and especially for my family, who had never seen me talk live. Their son, Thione Niang, was there. They were proud and moved to tears. Personally I didn't want to emulate anyone, because I wanted them to be better than me.

For me, this theater was a magical place, filled with memories. Among the hundreds of people there, one had a special significance for me. Tonton Sorano, who showed me the way when I was lost in Dakar ten years earlier, had come to hear me say a story in which he had such an important role. As soon as I saw the man with the special energy, I was felt immense gratitude. Although retired, Tonton Sorano had come to see me. I threw myself in his arms. I took off my wristwatch and gave it to him: "Tonton, keep it as a souvenir of the many moments spent here in Théâtre Sorano. This place was a great stage where we played several acts of my life and of our friendship." He said Thank you.

I went to that conference with what was needed to speak earnestly: my heart. I was so talkative that day! Maybe because I no longer had a watch on my wrist, I went way past my allotted time. At the end, in spite of pressing reminders from some Give1Project colleagues, I stayed in the Théâtre Sorano to take photos with the hundred young people still there. Those were always enriching little moments with each of them, during the photo.

It is always very sad for me when young people from various countries express desires, even basic ones, which are out of reach because of the way their country operates. Give1Project is a rallying cry for the emergence of young people, an exhortation so that everyone at their own level do one more step for themselves and for the advancement of mankind. The CEO of one of the largest academic entities in Senegal told me that he heard about our organization one day during a high-school meeting, when he noticed a few particularly bright, knowing and engaged students. His instant love for Give1Project led to the signature of an agreement between the two parties, and since then, thousands of high-school kids in his educational group registered freely to our melting-pot of exchanges, training and actions.

The goal of G1P is to create a new generation of citizens in each of the countries where we work to help build a better world. We must make up for the implicit abdication of certain governments and local officials. We hace a duty to be, as said Mahatma Gandhi, the change that we want to see in the world. This is what we aspire to when we clean up and refurbish the surroundings of my old elementary school in Senegal to make it better for the students, or when we plant trees in Niger to slow down desertification, or when we educate young people from Benin on the devastation of HIV and AIDS. We have installed business incubators for start ups in countries like Senegal where we support young entrepreneurs start businesses. The success in the entrepreneurship program surprised and inspired me to do even more. Young people in less than a year from ideas to hiring their first employees and interns was just encouraging.

We are in an exchange system where everybody wins: the young person who brings a project to the community and gets a chance to live in a better world.

Also this program has for some time been a real bonus for me: it allowed me to strengthen ties with my son Bass.

I love to watch as my eldest son, Bass, becomes a man. It fills me with joy to see him grow up by my side and join me in my mission to foster youth empowerment. In Paris, Bass was trained in photography and video editing, which he truly loves. Today, he is the official photographer of the Give1Project office. He travels around the world with my partners and I, recording all of our important moments. This year he directed his first documentary video, an informative and inspiring story about the Global Leadership Program 2014 in Washington, D.C.

You cannot imagine how proud I am to see my son understand what drives me every day and make use of that knowledge in his own life. Early on, I helped him understand that to be successful you must work, and that being the son of "such and such" a person is not enough. There will be hard times, when he'll believe there are no opportunities for him—and, it is in those moments that he will be able to use his strength to forge his own path with its own trajectory.

Also upon receiving his salary, Bass sends some to his mother, Anta, as I have always done for mine. We have agreed with each other that it's the right thing to do, and I'm proud that he believes it to be important.

When I look at all of the work we have done during these five years, with The Give1Project Team, I am impressed by the quantity and richness of all that has been achieved. I never imagined to accomplish so much in so little time. I never imagined to meet the many politicians and leaders of the business world and get as much support from them. I feel that we have really done what President Obama asked us to, we have continued to carry on this fantastic energy which brought us in his first election and which we again used during the second. And now my wish is to continue to use that energy to always go further and help transform the world day after day. Akon Lighting Afrika project we started in 2014 with Akon and Samba Bathily is proof that it is possible to go even further.

CHAPTER XIX

HERE WE GO AGAIN!

"In the middle of every difficulty lies opportunity." Albert Einstein

O ne year after his election, Barack Obama was as committed and determined as we could have hoped he'd be. He was working on the country's recovery by implementing the electoral promises made repeatedly over two long years spent campaigning. The American financial system was seized up, and the entire country was paralyzed. But "Doctor Obama" had the right profile and the infectious smile that reassures patients. The saying goes that when the doctor is optimistic, it is a good sign for the ill.

The economic recovery program had been generating fiery debates in the Senate as well as in the House. After it was finally adopted, this program was a booster for business activity. For us young people, it was a lifesaver for the future. I was still working in Congress advising on youth issues and worked alongside the Ohio delegate, Marcia Fudge. All delegates, in order to better understand what was going on in the field, had to attend conferences at the town hall. These conferences gave us the opportunity to hear firsthand from the ones most affected by President Obama's projects, the American people, and to learn about their expectations. The conferences also enabled Marcia Fudge to address her constituents during a meeting organized at Case Western University with an attendance of over a thousand people. Fudge was in favor of the Obama plan, but not all her supporters were. We opened the event with the introduction of ten young leaders from Cleveland who had been selected to be honored and receive awards. The idea was to avoid a brain drain by acknowledging their work and commitment; therefore motivating them enough that they would continue to do their best. I then introduced Marcia Fudge. She began her speech, but soon enough, was interrupted by Republicans and Tea Party supporters. Given the extreme level of their disruption, the police were called to remove several of them from the room and ensure safety for all.

Security has always been a big issue in the United States. It spares no social group, no racial group. While she was meeting her constituents in Arizona, elected Representative Gabrielle Giffords was the victim of a universally condemned attack. During a shooting rampage, she was shot in the head and six people were killed. She was first thought to have died, but a few minutes later it was revealed she had been very seriously injured in the attack. Long after, I was lucky enough to have dinner with Gabby Giffords and her husband. Although she recovered in a miraculous way, the attack considerably altered the course of her life. The aftermath of her wounds still make it difficult for her to walk and to talk. However, she soldiers on in the public eye and still fights for the American people, in addition to pursuing her efforts to end violence.

Regarding the economic recovery, President Obama has implemented a program costing roughly $789 billion, in order to create or save four million jobs. In March 2009, to counter the effects of the recession in the US, the Feds decided to buy $300 billion worth of US Treasury bonds, $750 billion worth of mortgage-backed securities (MBS), as well as $100 billion worth of liabilities from the Federal National Mortgage Association (Fannie Mae) and the Federal Home Loan Mortgage Corporation (Freddie Mac). These operations intended, among other things, to increase the volume of liquidities on the borrowing markets. The plan also included protectionist measures, allocating the financing of public equipment projects to companies that use manufactured goods made in the United States, a principle called the Buy American Provision.

After numerous battles and discussions, President Obama was able to sign a new law in March 2010. Public Law 111-148: Patient Protection and Affordable Care Act, also called "Obamacare," is highly debated even now. It is the largest and most important healthcare initiative in the United States since the 1965 creation of Medicare and Medicaid (respectively, health care for the elderly and for the poor).

Meanwhile, I was still the president in charge of international affairs for the Young Democrats. I was also cultivating my passion to serve the youth and to travel the world, telling all they can be master of their own destinies.

One of these opportunities was given to me by the US Department of State, which invited me to moderate a conference for young Belgians in Brussels. At the end of the event, the American ambassador invited me to his residence. Before being appointed, he had been an important supporter of President Obama's and had a role in the Democratic Party's finance committee. Believing the committee would be a good fit for me, he suggested I join. As soon as I got back to Washington, D.C., I visited the Democratic National Committee to find out how to join this group. I came to discover, however, that it was a closed entity, whose members were keen on preventing the entrance of newcomers.

One friend, a member of Gen 44 (an organization of young leaders under the age of forty working on the president's campaign), told me that Obama would announce his 2012 candidacy three weeks later in Washington. I was able to join the finance committee as the national co-chair of Gen 44. There was a lot of competition, because—but I would only find out the day before the event—the person who had raised the most funds would have the honor of introducing President Obama for the launch of the campaign.

Every night, the campaign managers would review the donations and amounts raised by each member of the committee. I was surprised to rank first with $14,000 in donations. It was my first time doing this, and fear of failure had kept me awake for more than two weeks. I had spent my sleepless nights sending emails and calling all my contacts. It was not an easy task—the president had lost some support, even among Democrats.

Some of his supporters thought he was too accommodating with the Republicans. He was also the culprit for the Democrat loss in the House, one year after his first election.

Obama was no longer the superstar he was in 2008, automatically cheered on at every appearance. He was the president who had to perform miracles. Yes, he was making progress on several fronts, but the crisis was at its peak and the American people were seeing none of the progress. They wanted a leader with magical powers, when the president believed more in them and their individual and collective capabilities than in magic. According to some very unhappy Americans, Obama was the source of all the hardship. Sometimes people would slam their door in my face to avoid hearing me defending Obama. However I never lost faith in my leader. I had encountered worse in 2007, and I knew it was possible to buck the trend and win the support of the disappointed by explaining that America was in better shape than before Obama's election.

The day before the launch of the 2012 campaign, I got a call from the director of Protocol who asked me to prepare a two-minute and fifty-five-second speech to announce the president and talk about our think tank, Gen 44. "This will prompt young people to better stand by the president," she said enthusiastically. It was indeed a fantastic opportunity. Beyond surprise, this news created a huge emotion in me, a real elation. I, the young Senegalese, arrived in the U.S. barely ten years before with only $20! I, little Thione Niang from Kaolack, was going to introduce the most powerful president in the world, before his candidacy to a second term. Emotions, sensations, and ideas were bustling in my mind. I had two minutes and fifty-five seconds to express my motivation and my commitment.

I would try to say only what really mattered. I took a moment to thank God. And as usual, I called my mother to ask her to pray for me. In order to find inspiration, I spent the night reviewing the speeches of past American presidents and reflected on the ideas and aspirations of Presidents Obama, Kennedy, and Clinton. These three minutes were completely absorbing me.

When I entered the Hilton Hotel, located just five minutes away from the White House, secret service and police personnel were already in place. Security was very tight. Sniffer dogs were used to detect possible weapons and other prohibited items. There was a long waiting line, mostly of donors who had come to support the president. The least expensive tickets were for students, who had to pay $44. There were also $250 tickets, $1,000 VIP tickets, and $10,000 tickets for those who wanted a photo with the president. Campaign members and honored guests had a separate entry.

About thirty minutes before the start of the event, a few of us went into a private room to greet the president, give him a brief update on our campaign efforts, and have our photo taken with him. This would be my ninth photo with President Barack Obama. He said hello, and asked about me. I replied that I was worried about the involvement of the young people in this campaign. "We have a big problem with the youth, they are not as enthusiastic as they were for the first campaign. We must do something."

"What do you suggest?" he asked.

"We have to create a mechanism to explain to the young voters what you have accomplished in the past few years, and how these achievements can positively impact their lives."

The president called his personal assistant Reggie Love, and asked him to see me to consider possible initiatives to gather massive support from the youth.

After this brief conversation and the photo shoot, I walked to the lectern where I had just been announced. My talk focused mostly on the importance of involving future American leaders alongside the president. "Tomorrow, what will you say when you are asked about what you did when Obama was fighting to change America and the world? Those who have understood and supported his vision, will be proud to say that we were with the president—that we were supporting him with all our youth and our drive."

The president then spoke about all the efforts initiated for the benefit of his fellow Americans, and about his unfailing commitment to the last great campaign of his political career. He was ready to win the White House for the second time. We were ready to reelect the one who best embodied the future of the United States. Over the next few months, we organized numerous fundraisers all over the country, often in the presence of the president and sometimes of Vice President Biden.

The day before the first presidential debate, our champion had a slight lead over Republican candidate Mitt Romney. The debate would be a real test that could confirm whether Romney had strong enough arguments to beat Obama. The debate was somewhat disappointing for our side, and it was a difficult moment for all the Democrats. Romney confirmed what we feared: he was a significant opponent.

A sliver of doubt had infiltrated our ranks and was weakening the mood. What to do when you know that the opponent is gaining ground in the polls? Even the most skeptical Republicans were becoming more and more confident about Romney, which made them bolder. There were two weeks of uncertainty and doubt in our ranks.

All of America was looking forward to the second debate, which would position the candidates before the actual vote. After the fundraising events, I was in back in Ohio, my familiar battleground. We couldn't win by resting in Washington. Each and every one of us had to go canvass each American voter.

I didn't get the support I was expecting from the constituents. I was visiting colleges, and during the door-to-door visits, it wasn't unusual to see doors close in my face. I remember a conversation with a forty-something woman, who said, "I voted for Obama in 2008, now I am disappointed and I don't plan on making the same mistake this time around."

"Why are you so categorical? I suggest we evaluate your expectations, and what Obama has done. If you are not convinced after that, I promise I won't insist."

"Evaluation? The evaluation I do it every day. When I open the fridge and I see no fresh food, or every time I can't take my kids to the doctor because it is too expensive. This is not a decision out of the blue. Even at church, we all had the same reaction when we spoke about the election. We all decided that we would no longer vote for Obama! Plus, he said he supported equal rights for marriage, even for homosexuals! No, no. With us, he doesn't stand a chance!"

Yes, Obama's timing was a risky one because that decision, made two months before the elections, was criticized by many religious lobbies and supporters. People lacked enthusiasm and were very worried about their own day-to-day issues, especially financial ones.

Many had lost their homes, because they just couldn't pay the rent or the mortgage.

There were many revealing encounters during this campaign. For example, I met a young man who said he didn't know there was an upcoming election. I couldn't believe it, but he was serious. "I am unemployed, and my wife left me six months ago—it's very hard for me to rise from the daily grind to follow the news. I take care of my little girl, who's five—that's all I care about." He asked me if he still had time to register to vote. But the election was only four days away and it was too late.

The second debate ended up being the turning point for the Democratic candidate. Obama's mission was to halt Romney's momentum. He did this beautifully, by being driven, proactive, convincing, and reassuring. At last, he used the weapons his supporters had longed for. He deflated Romney's arguments by depicting him as a multimillionaire who cares only about other multimillionaires, by recalling his extreme positions during the Republican primaries and, best of all, by evoking in his closing statement, Romney's claim it is the 47 percent of Americans who pay no taxes that would vote for Obama unequivocally.

For all the Democrats, that Tuesday night provided real relief.

I knew Ohio just as well as I knew Kaolack, and this helped me lead a real mobilization. On Election Day, we organized a gigantic gathering in front of the largest polling station in the state, to encourage our supporters to fulfill their civic duty. The influence of preachers and ministers, almost all black, was huge. They started operation "Praises to the Polls." As a matter of fact, most voters arrived around 1 p.m., dropped off by church buses. It was quite something to see long lines of people waiting in Cleveland's icy air, patiently spending hours there to go vote. They had faith in democracy. Blacks, whites, Latinos, Asians—they were all there. We members of the campaign organization were "rabatteurs": we would invite everyone to eat and drink after the vote, and we also had famous pop stars to entertain everyone. Stevie Wonder, John Legend, Vivica Fox, and other celebrities performed. Everything had to be done so that people would wait in line until it was their turn to vote. We knew that without Cuyahoga County, we couldn't win Ohio—and that without Ohio, we couldn't win the election. We gave it our all.

Ohio! As one of the swing states, Ohio was considered a key to unlocking the door of the White House. This thought gave us the strength to overcome all the difficulties. Two days before the election, the president visited six cities in a single day. This incredible campaign ended in Cleveland, a strategic city that the Democratic candidate visited nineteen times in all.

His last visit impressed his supporters in an unforgettable way: a last opportunity to get close with the Americans. On his way from Chicago to Washington, the president landed in front of 16,000 supporters waiting on the tarmac at Burke Lakefront Airport in Cleveland. They had waited for a long time, until eight o'clock at night. Air Force One, the presidential plane, moved slowly and stopped not too far from the crowd. The crowd was exhilarated when the president appeared, his sleeves rolled up. Thousands of smartphones immortalized the scene. Obama had lost his voice during the marathon of the previous few hours. When he called, "Hello, Cleveland!" his voice was faint—but the crowd heard him nonetheless and answered with cheers. At the end of his speech, Obama encouraged all to voice their opinions at the polling stations. Then he flew to Washington, D.C. All of Cleveland talked about his visit, and on social media, enthusiasm was at its peak.

Following calls to mobilization sent on Facebook and Twitter, some friends of mine from New York and Washington had arrived to help me through the last days of the campaign. We bonded over high solidarity and great team spirit. Within this orchestra, the moves and motions we had practiced so often had made each of us a virtuoso perfectly playing his part.

After the vote, the results came in. Initially we had been poorly positioned because Mitt Romney was leading in many cities. There was a flurry of worried text messages. "What is going on?" I too was wondering. Hundreds of supporters were attending the "watch party" I had organized in Cleveland. Our focus was on CNN, BBC, FOX—we were jumping from one channel to the next to find more reassuring news, but in vain.

At 11 p.m., the Ohio results were finally announced. They would reflect our eagerness to fight. Even though our mobilization had gone beyond the limits of the state, Ohio would be the measuring stick of our success. Ohio appeared in blue on the voter map graphic, which meant Obama had won the state. The crowd screamed with happiness. My phone rang through the night with calls from all parts of the world.

The party continued while we waited for Mitt Romney's concession speech, which would signal the official end of the political contest. The Republican candidate took a long time to give his statement, which was explained when he later told the press that he had prepared only one speech: a victory speech. Obama then made his appearance, victorious yet humble, and joyful about his continued service to the American people.

On multiple occasions, this experience has served me. It is well known that the re-election of President Obama was hard fought. We dared to be optimistic, visualizing positive outcomes. Do not let yourself become tainted by the doubts of others. Always focus on solutions, with daring optimism. I have maintained this perspective since.

CHAPTER XX

AN IMPORTANT STEP FORWARD TO THE FUTURE: AKON LIGHTING AFRICA.

"In this bright future you can't forget your past" Bob Marley

Every September, I organized a seminar on Leadership in the White House, the "Global Leadership Program," and that since President Obama took office. I invite young "leaders", members of Give1Project, from everywhere around the world. They are entrepreneurs, writers, politicians, activists ect…

In 2013, I contacted the Senegalese-American star Akon to intervene in the program. What a pleasant surprise to see him accept it!

I have rarely met a person as humble as Akon. In an exemplary simplicity, he can adapt to any situation. I saw him in many contexts always keep calm.

He was the surprise guest of the reception that my great friend François Delattre, Ambassador of France in Washington 2010 until 2014, organized in my honor, bringing together 60 young leaders from 28 countries. A great gift for all participants!

During a discussion with Akon, I asked him what he thought we should do for Africa, our homeland. Being from there, we feel obligated to make our contribution to the building and the construction and development of the African continent.

— "Akon, imagine the use that would have Luther King or Mandela had they had at their disposal Twitter, Facebook or Instagram! I told him.

— You Akon, you have 52 million people who follow you on Facebook, more "followers" than President Obama. What are you going to do about this opportunity to influence lives? What memories would you leave? Beyond the music, that tomorrow will tell you, your children, your grandchildren and their children?

— You and me, we have a responsibility towards Africa, that of giving hope to the African youth. Very few young Africans have the opportunity that you and I have had. We've traveled all over the world, much has been seen, heard and understood.

— Now it's up to us to create opportunities for young people. So are working together for a cause greater than both of us, to influence the world. "

In agreement with this idea, Akon then spoke to me of a Sheikh he met in Bahrain and their talks to invest in energy in Africa. They needed somebody like me to handle government relations. The Sheikh wanted letters of invitations from 7 African countries (Senegal, Guinea Conakry, Burkina Faso, Gabon, Mali, Sierra Leone, Equatorial Guinea) and established by their Presidents in person.

Government relations being my specialty, I pledged then to meet and persuade the presidents of seven countries (Senegal, Guinea Conakry, Burkina Faso, Gabon, Mali, Sierra Leone, Equatorial Guinea) I already knew to collect the invitation letters.

Sheikh and its partners needed to come to Africa with us and invest in "power plans". During three long weeks, I traveled to Africa to meet one by one the heads of state to obtain these invitation letters signed of their hand. After multiple conference calls, Sheikh began to hesitate, when I received urgent calls from the presidents asking the date of our arrival.

I felt falter Sheikh interest to invest in Africa ... I called Akon and told him of my desire to protect our reputation as original Africans. We had to find a solution outside of the Sheikh. Akon agreed and asked me to consider what follow. I offered to find an expert on energy issues, a major problem in Africa. Both him and I have no background on energy.

I remembered having met in Conakry a year earlier, a young Malian named Samba Bathily. Samba worked a lot with the Chinese on infrastructure in Africa but also on the issue of energy solar.

I received Samba in my Give1Project office in Dakar and he came with two of his Chinese partners on another subject. I mentioned Akon and I project to work on energy in Africa. Samba couldn't believe that it was the same Akon I was talking about. The name Akon acted as a sesame. Through conversations, the solar solution has emerged.

At night I talked to Akon and asked him to come and meet me and Samba in Dakar to move forward. A week later Akon came directly from the airport to local Give1Project office in Dakar. We locked in my office for 7 long hours and "Akon Lighting Africa" and Solektra International were created.

We came up with Akon Lighting Africa name. The logo, website and communication materials have been found by young Give1Project, stayed to work on these issues during a creative night.

Then we went to see the Presidents starting with Senegal, our homeland. 10 countries in 10 days, the meeting of Heads of

States, their energy ministers but also young people organized by Give1Project. In each country, I motivated young people to be involved in the solar project.

We went to the largest university in each country at the meeting of Youth, and the crowds were amazing. African youth was mobilizing with us to rebuild Africa. Give1Project structures in each country were organizing everything before we arrived, and my previous years of travel involving youth in different countries proved very useful.

Today, we are present in 14 African countries and aim to be in 38 total. Millions of homes have been electrified and the lives of their inhabitants change every day. Even today, 600 million Africans have no access to electricity; we are about to give them energy.

Certainly, it is ambitious, but with work, it is the necessary condition for achieving unimaginable goals for many of us.

In the most remote villages of Kenya, for example in Masai country was electrified, gave light to people who in life had never seen. In villages in Senegal, Benin, Mali, Burkina Faso, Gabon, Niger etc., we give the opportunity to thousands of young Africans to install solar panels and maintain them.

During our negotiations, our Chinese partners wanted to impose their technicians for installation. Speaking, I served my disagreement: "We need a project manager and a controller, for the rest I think Africa has enough young people who need to work." On the same time, young people are trained to install the panels and residing there, they could also provide maintenance if necessary.

I convinced my two partners, Samba and Akon, and our Chinese partners have relented.

Today, Akon Lighting Africa is employing thousands of young Africans. Imagine the turmoil: access to electricity allows students, pupils and students to study after dark, or doctors and midwives to care for the sick without waiting for the next day, luck of light to intervene.. ..

Because my role was to manage relationships with governments and institutions on the one hand, and mobilizing the youth on the other hand, I went to New York to meet with UN officials.

After many meetings, a partnership with the Office "Sustainable Energy for All" was established, and we were invited to the energy summit at the UN in May 2015. Akon, Samba and I went to New York.

In the presence of Heads of State, Ministers, entrepreneurs from the private energy sector from around the world, I opened the conference.

In my youthful dreams and my ambitions of the time, the UN held a special place in my ambitions then. Schoolboy in Kaolack, I looked Koffi Anan, Secretary General at the time of the UN, deliver his speech, standing on the platform where the UN General Assembly members expressed Presidents. And 25 years later I realized this dream by presenting a project whose aim is to bring light to millions of young people studying in craft lamps or street lamps around the world. It was my turn to speak and share my ambitions and dreams with the world. My dreams for the youth of the world, especially that of Africa.

We are children of the continent, and simply we need to be faster than the sun continually: life at home stops at sunset. That is to say that the production and schoolwork stop, the streets become dangerous, particularly for women and children, basic medical services are interrupted. Leaving Africa, living elsewhere, we have seen how electricity contributes to innovation, education and creativity. Back in our villages, all three of us have found children read or do their homework by candlelight! The situation was unbearable.

The needs are enormous: over 600 million people in Africa are still in the dark each night. Inhabited by a sixth of the world population, Africa receives only four percent of the energy supply in the world! The situation is even more unbearable when you realize that energy is the condition for development. The energy means everything: access to water, access to health, education, media, culture.

Far beyond the sole energy that generates jobs, business, administration, growth in short.

With our solar solutions, we can radically change lives and economies. The hardest part is to convince others to share what you believe. As President Mandela said, "It always seems impossible until it is done." We did it: we showed that we can accelerate the electrification of Africa and we were right to be ambitious! And we convince with a strong argument: our business model.

At the United Nations, we announced the creation of our solar academy in Mali . First of its kind on the continent, the center will be open to all Africans wishing to invest in the solar sector and will provide them with vocational training.

The Solar Academy will have the support of the international Solektra; some of our international partners will provide the equipment and ensure the training program. It will be specialized in the installation and maintenance of solar electrification systems, with special emphasis on micro-grids currently booming, especially in rural areas.

We have the sun(320 days of sunshine a year), we have innovative technologies for domestic and collective electrification; now, it is the need to strengthen African expertise. This is the mission we set for ourselves. We are investing in more than energy alone: we invest in human capital. We can accelerate the transformation of our continent provided that as of now generations of engineers, technicians and skilled African entrepreneurs.

Only with a real economic approach that we can make the difference. We have demonstrated that the private sector is able to provide solutions and to grow much faster than development aid.

I believe we can move from the paradigm of "development by Aid" to that of "fair trade" with robust and reliable contractors, then the world will have easier access to the ideas and talents from the new generation of African youth. That is why I am committed to this project to help bring energy to the heart of Africa with my partners Akon and Samba. It is a personal commitment, rooted in personal memories, one of those mornings when my grandfather woke me up very early before school to finish the job that I had not managed to do at night for lack of light .

Chapter XXI

EVERYTHING IS POSSIBLE!

*"There are those who look at things the way they are, and ask why...
I dream of things that never were, and ask why not?" Robert Kennedy*

In early July 2015, I was invited to a private dinner with President Barack Obama, in Beverly Hills, California at the home of filmmaker Tyler Perry.. On this occasion I had a long discussion with him. I felt the need to talk with him on some points, particularly on immigration law, the "My Brother's Keeper" initiative, the United States Agency for International Development's (USAID) "Power Africa" initiative, and the work I am doing with African-American singer and activist Akon to promote access to energy in Africa.

I also spoke with President Obama about the recent meeting I'd had with his team about Power Africa at the USAID office in Washington. During the meeting, I'd stressed the advantages of a partnership between "Akon Lighting Africa" and "Power Africa." Now, congratulating the president on his decision to travel to Kenya for the Global Entrepreneur Summit, he invited me to the summit, calling his aide over to take down my information and send me an invitation per his instructions. Two days later, on a Sunday afternoon, I received an invitation from the White House on behalf of the president to join him in Kenya at the Global Entrepreneurship Summit. (The year before, I had given a speech at the Summit's closing meeting in Morocco, presided over by Vice President Joe Biden.) Three weeks later, there I was in Kenya with Akon to give the opening GES speech in Nairobi.

At the summit, entrepreneurs from all sectors represented 120 countries. When I spoke, I spoke of our actions, not only why and how we carry them out, but especially about their impact on the African continent. Akon's words were also motivating and inspiring.

The Kenyan people greeted President Obama enthusiastically on this trip to his father's homeland. At the official State dinner, the president made a speech, recounting his trip to Kenya ten years before in search of his family and roots. This time around, it was Obama's sister, not his father, who met and welcomed him at the Nairobi airport—and this time, she was greeting the president of the United States of America. The emotion and energy in the room were palpable and touching.

That night was very memorable for me; the presence of President Obama's paternal grandmother, his sister, and other family members was a strong symbol. I also left with a enduring pride about my former boss, Congresswoman Marcia Fudge, who accompanied President Obama on this trip to Kenya, along with twenty other senators and members of Congress.

At that moment, I realized again that everything is possible!

CHAPTER XXII

A LETTER TO MY GRANDFATHER

An intimate reflection of enormous gratitude to my dearest late grandfather

"The elephant dies, but its tusks remain."
African proverb

My mind keeps returning to the last time I saw you. It was at the party celebrating the end of Ramadan, three months before you passed away. You mentioned a dream that made me sad. I remember exactly the way you described it: "I saw my face on the side of the moon. Spiritually, it means that God will call me up quite soon."

You wiped my tears and explained that my role was to take care of the family. You then gave me a large piece of fabric, about 6 yards long that would serve as your burial shroud. You handed me the legal papers regarding the house, and gave me your watch as a gift. This watch had enormous sentimental value for you because you had brought it back from Mecca where you made a pilgrimage in

1978, the year I was born. "The day I leave this world, I want you to be near me when they put me in the ground and cover me with soil," you said.

On October 18, 1998, at 6 p.m. in Dakar, I was reaching the end of my evening prayer when my cousin Sheikh Diop announced in a distressed voice that I had to go home right away. I feared something awful had happened. At the house, your sister Mam Khady was crying. Sobbing, she confirmed my fears: "Your grandfather wants you in Kaolack immediately," she said.

"Has Grandfather left us?"

"No...no," she said, averting her eyes. I was not convinced. The darkness in Kaolack seemed thicker than usual that night. A few steps away from the house, I heard shouting and crying.

When I stepped inside, my uncle Pape Diouf sent me to town, saying I had to get a loan that was needed to prepare the mourning. He took the fabric from my hands and told me to hurry. I had no idea that this was a trick to expedite your burial ceremony while I was away. Maybe it was to spare me the sadness of seeing you gone forever. Regardless, it was one of the most painful moments in my life.

Back in Kaolack, the convoy made its way to Touba, the burial place. My aunts shouted when they saw I'd returned and told me to hurry to Touba. That two-hour trip was the longest one in my life.

All I could think about was your last will and your wish that I be near you when your body was to be buried. I prayed not to miss that moment. Once in Touba, I saw the entire family at the cemetery gates. Unfortunately the burial had just ended, and I was the only one who had not made it there in time, even though you had insisted I be there that day. I rushed to your tomb, in a swirl of dust, in front of the crowd. I was intent on paying you a last tribute before soil would cover you forever. I got down next to you in the tomb. I couldn't imagine life without you, my constant source of inspiration and courage. I begged you to not leave me, as if you could come back to life at will. I don't know how you did it, but right then you conveyed the message that everything I needed was already in me. I don't know how, but I saw your serene smile fade away in a swirl of dust. Then I noticed the emptiness.

My cousins tried to comfort me and led me to the house, where I settled in your room to pray, meditate, and cry. My pain became indescribable when I learned from my cousin Ndeye Khady that you had died in the worst possible manner. Grandfather, I have never healed from the fact that you died of starvation. It is a truth that is difficult to accept. Cousin Ndeye was with you during your final hours, and said that five days went by without you having any food. We were used to being hungry at home, and you even more than us. You would always say that not eating made your faith stronger, but now I know you were being strong for us.

I will stay true to the promise I have made to you—to take care of the family and beyond that to play a role in the evolution of society in everyday life. This is one of the reasons for my commitment to the development and empowerment of youth. I wish that all people could express themselves as fully as possible, and that everyone could realize their talents and travel the paths that are their own.

In 2015, I went to Mecca in order to make my Umrah; and at each stage, you were at my side. Your radiant presence beside me, I remembered that you had been in the same place, making your Umrah the year I was born. It was a source of joy to me, and right then, I breathed in a new desire to continue your actions for the good of all. May you be thanked for all that you gave me—it has allowed me to become the person I am today.

CHAPTER XXIII

A STUBBORN OPTIMISM

« *Regardless of where the wind blows, the sun always goes where it must* ». *African proverb*

I n a crowd in Tokyo, Japan, a young man once told me, as many of his fellows had in other countries, that we live in a century where nothing is planned for the youth. He asked me what advice I could provide about this situation, which he deemed catastrophic. I answered that it is a formidable opportunity. Not everyone has a chance to design his destiny based on his own aspirations. « Take your life in your own hands and shape it according to your aspirations; if you encounter no difficulty, it means that you have undertaken nothing worthy».

The words accomplishment, success, and wealth show no preference for a particular skin color. Whether you are black, white, or yellow, you can find role models who have been successful in all fields. We live in a century where you don't need a mine or an oil rig to make a fortune. You just need an idea. Your mind is the most fantastic gold mine and the most providential oil rig. Therefore we are all rich. But some of us choose to keep their mine unexploited, or to exploit only a tiny fraction of it. Those who decide to fully use their mine will innovate, create, and surprise the world; then they will be surprised to be considered geniuses, because in truth they are not! They are only miners who have dug a little further than the others. Think like a miner, keep digging! Do not stop at the sand that covers the mine, because sand is a commodity that grants you nothing special. Go beyond the obvious. Be someone special.

This is not an invitation to walk the same path I walked, but to follow yours with enthusiasm and bravery. It is an invitation to walk towards a better tomorrow, as years ago I promised myself I would. Nature warns us of what it holds for us: sometimes it rains, or thunder roars, or the sky is full of clouds, but none of these phenomenon prevents the sun from rising and from following its course. You are the sun that must rise in spite of the clouds. The effort is never lost, but sometimes it is we who give up too soon. On the path to self-realization, there are must-have companions, whose names are: faith, perseverance, audacity, tolerance, forgiveness, openness, patience.

I do not claim I know everything about the world, nor do I claim I can address all your concerns, because, just like you, I am still walking on my way to a better tomorrow. But my secret lies in the following simple truth: I will not encourage you to follow me but rather to do like me by carving your own path as best as you can to get to your own destination.

In those moments where despair tempts you, try to remember that what you do, you don't do only for yourself but also for your parents, your close circle, your town, your country. You do it for the young people in the world. By overcoming the difficulties, by taking another step forward, you help the youth in the world. Therefore you help the world. You give a sense to your life. Success is never complete if it is only for you. We have a duty to leave the world a better place than it was when we found it, for the next generations.

An essential question that one must ask though: What is success? The right answer is the one that you provide yourself. Success is a relative concept which evaluation depends on each person's aspirations. But I agree with President Obama who says that "if your only ambition in life is to get rich, then you are not ambitious." From my small experience, I drew strong and unmovable beliefs. Here is a saying by Martin Luther King that strongly impacted me: "Take the first step in faith. You don't have to see the whole staircase, just take the first step."

When in doubt or in despair, try to stop and remember that you are not alone. Somewhere, far away or close by, there is a Mam Thione, someone who puts his trust and unconditional support in you.

I was able to get on the right path because I was lucky to meet people who had a desire to serve, and who served me. Also, my drive to get ahead was stronger than the various reasons that were dragging me downwards. Serving others is the most noble and most enriching activity. It is an occupation that tolerates no bitterness, no hate, and no vengeance. One must cultivate forgiveness and purity of mind to understand human beings. Strengthened by this ambition, I made a clean slate of all the conflicts with my family, my father, some brothers and sisters. The decision to tell my story is not fueled by some form of exhibitionism, but by the desire to share my hopes with the greatest number. An overflowing optimism drives me, and forces me to share with others. An overflowing optimism regarding our future, we who are the young of the world. I strongly believe that the best way to get rich is to share.

Share always, especially when we think there is nothing to give.

ACKNOWLEDGEMENTS

I owe a great many thanks to a great many people who helped and supported me during the writing of this book.

First of all, I am grateful to God for establishing me to complete this book.

To Mam Thione and Mother, it's impossible to thank you adequately for everything you've done,
from loving me unconditionally to raising me and instilled
traditional values and taught me humility, faith and kindness to everyone. I could not
have asked for better role-models.

And to my cousins Ndeye Khady, Ndeye Diakhou, Ousseynou, Bouna, Diodio, Awa Diouf and Thiéka, thanks for all of the wonderful memories of growing up, and for your continued support and encouragement. A special thank you to Ralph for showing me that anything is possible with faith, hard work and determination.

Above all, I want to thank my mom, my two sons Bass and El Haji, and the rest of my family who supported and encouraged me in spite of all the time it took me away from them. It was a long and difficult journey for them. A special thank you to my brother Falou and Amadou who have always been there for me.

I would like to express my gratitude to my editor Naida Wesley:) Bongo who provided support, talked things over, read, wrote, offered comments, and assisted in the editing, proofreading and time in polishing this book. I am extremely grateful and indebted to her for her expert, sincere and valuable guidance and encouragement she extended to me.

I am most grateful to Didier and Alix who have put countless hours to edit the french version of the book. Their believe in me have touched me great deal. I am thankful you are in my life. Without the two of you we wouldn't have a short version. Your advices and critics will always be valuable to me.

Rama and Aminata my very first readers and constant champions throughout the
writing process, thank you for all of the feedback. Thanks for believing in me and always on my side to make things better.

I also place on record, my sense of gratitude to one and all who, directly or indirectly, have their helping hand in this venture, Jacqueline Cofield, Ashsley Causey, My brother Amour Gbovi, from Benin, Mor and Daouda Ndao, My brother Elhadji Falou Niang and my dearest friend Amadou Gningue, Joyana Niang, Tonton Sorano Ibrahima Diakhate, Sam Tidmore of Cleveland, Michael Ruff, Fatima Niang, Councilman Kevin Conwell, Senator Shirley Smith, Cheikh Baye Touty Niass, Same Tidmore, Dr. Corttrelle Kinney, Momo Diallo, Amour Avoce, Karen Andre, Steven Olikara, Ass Dieng and Oumy Salamata Niass who opened his doors for me in my first days in the US, Jennifer Douglas my American mother, Ben Niass, Tarik, Al Housseynou Ba, Deidré Davis, My brother Mamadou Niang, Tonton Pape Diop, Dr. Corttrell Kinney, Anta Dieye, tante Sadio, Tante Nabou and Tante Mbegou, President Obama for his inspiration, Al Housseynou Ba. My entire Give1Project Family around the world, they inspire me daily.

Printed in Great Britain
by Amazon